While It Is Day

While It Is Day

An Autobiography

Elton Trueblood

HARPER & ROW, PUBLISHERS
New York, Evanston, San Francisco, London

WHILE IT IS DAY: *An Autobiography.* Copyright © 1974 by Elton Trueblood. All rights reserved. Printed in the United States of America. No part of this book may be used or reproduced in any manner whatsoever without written permission except in the case of brief quotations embodied in critical articles and reviews. For information address Harper & Row, Publishers, Inc., 10 East 53rd Street, New York, N.Y. 10022. Published simultaneously in Canada by Fitzhenry & Whiteside Limited, Toronto.

Designed by Janice Stern

Library of Congress Cataloging in Publication Data
Trueblood, David Elton, 1900-
    While it is day.

    1. Trueblood, David Elton, 1900-   I. Title.
BX7795.T75A37   289.6′092′4 [B]   73–18680
ISBN 0–06–068741–X

Contents

"We must work the works of him who sent me, while it is day. . . ."

—*John 9:4*

Preface

Every man's life, thought Dr. Samuel Johnson, may be best written by himself. However difficult it may be to achieve objectivity, each person possesses information hidden from any outside observer. Though the difficulties of autobiographical writing are both immense and obvious, the advantages are correspondingly great because the ultimate evidence is that of witness.

During nearly all of my adult life I have been consciously grateful to many who have provided firsthand testimony concerning their own lives. Starting with student days I have valued works of this type, believing with Leslie Stephen that autobiography is "the most fascinating type of literature." Ever since the time when I shared in a famous Harvard course in seventeenth-century religious prose, the classics in this field have been my prized possessions. Among these are the memoirs of Richard Baxter, George Fox, and many others of their century, but I have not limited my reading of such works to this flowering period. I have been also drawn to the autobiographical writings of Benjamin Franklin, John Woolman, John Stuart Mill, and many more.

Any person who understands his own imperfection is naturally hesitant to write about his own life, but serious thought will make him realize that this is no absolute deterrent, since each one has something worth sharing. Here Dr. Johnson's wisdom applies: "I have often thought," wrote Johnson, "there has rarely passed a life of which a judicious and faithful narrative would not be useful." If the Rambler was right, no elaborate justification is required. Every life is short, and the best of human knowledge is slight, but there is great merit in trying to tell what has actually transpired. The most artful tale, once it is known to be false, cannot compete in interest with the faithful report of an actual life, no matter how modest it may be.

Of autobiographies produced in our own century, the one that has appealed to me most is *Pilgrim's Way* by Lord Tweedsmuir. This book has provided me something of a model, demonstrating the possibility of an autobiography that is primarily topical. I soon saw that my own life could best be understood with reference to the different vocations which I have pursued simultaneously. Consequently, in the book which I have written, there is no attempt at a strict chronological order.

To tell what he has tried to do, and how he has tried to think, may be the most important service which one person can render to another. As we all walk essentially the same path, we stumble the less if our predecessors have left a few markers. It is the duty of each person who has profited from some guidance to leave a few markers of his own. That is why this book has been written. It is an effort to pay my toll on a road which others have constructed.

In his famous opening, dated 1580, Montaigne wrote, "I am myself the matter of my book." Much as I admire Montaigne, I cannot say the same about my own book. It has of course been impossible to avoid the use of the first person singular, but, as I have written, I have been thinking chiefly of those who have helped me. Therefore, this is not really a book about one person, but about many persons. There have been numerous forks in the road, but at each of these there has been someone to point the way. Thus this book is fundamentally a record of my indebtedness. Though most of those to whom I am indebted are now beyond my power to repay, I can at least acknowledge what it is that I owe and try to make payment in the only coin that is available.

E.T.

While It Is Day

1. Child

For the first time, perhaps, since that land emerged from geologic ages, a human face was set toward it with love and yearning.

Willa Cather

The pioneering habit of my family began more than two hundred years before I was born, the first big journey being by ship from London to what is now Elizabeth City, North Carolina. On an old Carolina map the word Trueblood appears where Elizabeth City now stands. John and Agnes Trueblood arrived in North Carolina in 1682, he being of a Lincolnshire family and she, Agnes Fisher, coming from the vicinity of Swarthmore Hall, the home of George Fox. The pair met and were married at Devonshire House, London, on the 5th month (now July), 31, 1679, both giving as their local address, Shoreditch. Because Quaker records were kept so meticulously, we are able to read their marriage certificate now. All of their four children were born in America.

The progeny of that one remarkable pair are so numerous that a published book about them fills 287 closely printed pages. The reader may understand something of the multiplication of offspring when I say that my grandfather, Oliver, was the eighth child of Caleb II, who was the fourteenth child of Caleb I. Even more fantastic is the fact that when she was born, my daughter, Elizabeth, was, on her mother's side, the one hundred sixty-seventh descendant of a living woman.

Most of the descendants of John and Agnes Trueblood have demonstrated the mobility for which America is famous, helping to start new communities in several states, but the normal movement has been in only one direction, west. It came to me as a distinct shock in my early manhood when I suddenly realized that by moving east, I was reversing a process that had continued for nearly three hundred years. It is with deep emotion that I have visited the Lincolnshire village of Beckingham where my people lived before their westward trek began. The village was the home of Arnold Trueblood, who died in Lincoln Castle in 1658, persecuted for his Quaker nonconformity. When, in London, I first encountered the record of this, I felt keenly the magnitude of my indebtedness. The record, *A Collection of the Sufferings of the People Called Quakers*, reads, "Anno 1658. Arnold Trueblood was committed to Lincoln Gaol for Tithes, and after many Weeks Confinement died there."

For more than a century nearly all of the Truebloods of America lived in the area north of Albemarle Sound. They belonged to a strong Quaker community which was visited by traveling ministers, one of whom was John Woolman, of *Journal* fame, who came first in 1746 and later in 1757. The home of my ancestor, Amos Trueblood, was a natural place of abode for these eloquent and thoughtful visitors. One result was that the members of the community, including my ancestors, realizing almost a century before the Emancipation Proclamation that slavery was a sin, liberated their many slaves when that was a highly unpopular action to take. The plight of former slaves was one of the chief reasons for the second migration of most of the Trueblood family to the Northwest Territory in the first two decades of the nineteenth century. We know, for example, that my great-grandfather's sister, Laetitia, wife of John Smith, in 1806 an original settler of Richmond, Indiana, transported all of her liberated slaves to Indiana in order to establish them in newly created industries. If she had not done so, they might have been rounded up and resold. My great-grandfather, Caleb II, who was the first of several Truebloods to settle in Washington County, Indiana, is buried in the Blue River cemetery, near Salem, where many of the former slaves are likewise buried.

While the first Trueblood trek was by ship and the second by covered wagon, the third family trek, immediately after the Civil War, was mostly by train. The first through passenger train arrived in Des Moines, Iowa, on the evening of September 9, 1867. The railroad, later called the Rock Island, was destined to open an entire area to new settlers, including my own grandparents. With southern Indiana already crowded, so far as agriculture was concerned, the fabulous unspoiled land beyond the Mississippi was enticing to young families. Oliver and Mary Trueblood sold their eighty-acre farm near Salem, Indiana, and with the proceeds were able to purchase one hundred sixty acres of land on the eastern edge of Warren County, Iowa. It was land which had never been plowed, lying in a township where, with not a single tree, the prairie seemed endless in extent.

By the time Oliver and Mary reached Iowa the train to Des Moines had been operating eighteen months, but the facilities were meager. With their five children, one of them only four months old, they had to sit in the station all night, without a fire, their only food being that which they had brought with them on the train. In the morning Oliver's nephew, Charles Trueblood, came to take the family south to Indianola where Charles was already established. In spite of having hot bricks in the sled, Mary, who was always frail, was terribly chilled upon their arrival at Indianola and had to be carried into the house. A few days later the Oliver Truebloods reached their new home on the prairie. Like the other settlers they suffered from heat in summer as well as cold in winter, and in case of sickness they were far removed from any medical assistance. On July 1 of that first difficult summer the baby, John Allen, died and was buried in the first grave of the new community. The grave, now flanked by those of my father and mother, established the location of the meetinghouse. When sufficient wood was available, Oliver built a fence about the grave.

For his quarter section of land Oliver Trueblood paid $2,770 in cash. That was possible because in the autumn of 1868 he had received $3,200 for his debt-free farm near Salem, Indiana. The new farm was midway between South River and White Breast, both of which were bordered by timber, though the land between the streams was all prairie. Timber along the rivers provided fence posts, but most of the material for building houses had to be brought from sawmills at a considerable distance. Without any wood to burn in stoves, the new residents of the pioneer settlement survived the cold winters only because of the coal mines ten miles southeast, along White Breast River. The deposit of coal in that area soon attracted miners from Wales, including the parents of John L. Lewis, later to become the head of the United Mine Workers, who was born at Lucas, Iowa, February 12, 1880. Forty years after the arrival of the first settlers my father was still hauling our winter's coal from a mine to which I often accompanied him. It was our practice to leave home at 5 a.m. in order to be among those on hand with their wagons when the day's coal, pulled out of the mine by a burro, began to emerge from the shaft.

On the quarter section which Oliver purchased there was already a small house, with one room above another and a lean-to kitchen attached. Food was of course very scarce. There was as yet no cultivated fruit, and milk was a rarity. Oliver rode the prairie for weeks before he was able to purchase a milk cow and thus provide for his little children. There was corn bread, but bread made from wheat was available only on great occasions.

One of Oliver's two good horses was bitten on the leg by a rattlesnake and could never pull a load again, but Father, as a small boy, rode the crippled horse to the post office seven miles away to collect the mail both for his mail-hungry parents and their neighbors.

Though the land was beautiful to see, there was much back-breaking work before it could become productive. The only hope of survival, of course, was the willingness of the pioneers to help one another, which they did magnificently. Since most of the residents were Quakers, they met in my grandfather's house during the first summer and organized their community, to which they gave the appropriate name, Waveland. My father, Samuel, was then three years old.

In parts of Warren County, particularly those near Middle River, there was abundant hardwood, some of which is preserved to this day, but the hauling of it presented a serious problem. The horses were overworked, and when one died, the replacement became a major financial problem. Fences soon became a necessity if the new crops, produced with such difficulty, were to be protected from wandering cattle. Grandfather was able to get fence posts by bringing them thirty miles from the Des Moines River. My mother, with her parents, David and Lydia Crew, arrived five years later than the Truebloods and settled one mile from them. Because David Crew had been a carpenter in Chesterhill, Ohio, he was quickly able, not only to build his own three-room house, but also to help others with their own structures. Maple seeds sent from Ohio were planted in rows in order to start seedlings, which my mother, riding her pony, carried to the new neighbors for miles around.

As soon as possible the pioneers erected, in addition to their own houses, the place of worship and the place of learning. In 1869, the year my family arrived, Warren County Friends established Ackworth Academy about twelve miles from the home of my grandparents. A two-story structure was built of bricks which the men burned on the academy ground. They named the institution Ackworth, for the oldest of Quaker schools in Yorkshire, and purchased books with a generous gift of $1,000 sent by English Friends. Three years later those same brave people joined others in establishing what we know as William Penn College. How could they, having so little, undertake so much? The real wonder lies in what those Friends of a century ago considered necessary. The schools were necessary, they thought, not for survival, but for the kind of life to which they were devoted. They could have kept their bodies alive without the academy and the college, but they had concern for more than bodies.

Both my father and mother enrolled in Ackworth Academy, cooking for themselves as the other students did. Fortunately for us, both of our parents cherished autograph books, which still exist and by which we can verify dates and names. On January 15, 1883, when Mother was fifteen, one boy, Elton Trimble, wrote in her book, "Forget me not. Your darling." In Father's book there is a note to "Sammy," signed by Effie Crew.

Father's time as a student at the academy was much shorter than Mother's because he was needed on the farm for the greater part of each year. Oliver's health was not good, and as it steadily worsened, he had to take his teen-age son with him so that the two together could make one "hand." In cradling the wheat there were normally four men, operating on the four sides of a square, but on Oliver Trueblood's farm it had to be four men and a boy. It is clear now, as we look at the record, that the family took advantage of Sam's good nature and worked him too hard. Finally, Oliver and Mary told him that they were willing to send him away for an advanced education, but he replied that the offer had come too late because he had other plans. Already he was thinking of Effie, the only child of David Crew, and was about to buy a horse of his own. He could do that because he was employed by various neighbors and was permitted to keep half of his earnings, the other half going to his parents as long as he was single.

Effie Crew was an ideal companion for my father. She could do any work that a man could do, and she could sew and cook equally well. Leaving the academy at seventeen, she secured a license to teach and soon had a position in a school in which some of the pupils were older than she was. She rode her horse to the school each day and helped her parents each evening.

The most interesting phase of the courtship of Sam and Effie is their unusual practice of keeping a joint diary, in which they continued to write after their marriage. Most of the diary is in Father's handwriting, but, even before they were married, Mother wrote some of it. On March 24, 1889, one day after Father's twenty-third birthday, the account tells us that he went "with Dick Wright to the Catholic Church." The experience was of course utterly foreign to anything that the young men had known previously. Four days later he wrote, "Bought a plow for $8.00." On April 13 we learn that Effie had the mumps, and the next day, "Went to see my patient again tonight." Though there is no word of engagement, they must have had some kind of understanding by the spring of 1889. In any case they were married in November, after Father had harvested his crop of corn. To help the young couple as they began life together, Oliver and Mary gave them one horse and a wagon, all they could spare.

My parents began their married life in a tiny house on forty acres between the two homesteads. They had a little furniture, including the walnut dresser which Mother had bought for eighteen dollars, her first month's pay as a teacher. In January 1890 they made their first important purchase, a Seth Thomas clock. It now sits on the mantel of my study, having operated for more than eighty-three years without once being repaired. I can hear it ticking as I write.

In January 1891 Effie bore the first of five children, my older brother, Oscar, now a retired merchant residing in Ames, Iowa. A second child, Blanche, was born in the same house about two years later. The little girl brought wonderful joy to her mother, making the blow of her death on July 27, 1895, almost unbearable. Sam and Effie continued to write in their joint diary for more than five years after their marriage, but with the death of Blanche the writing came to an abrupt end. On July 8, 1895, Father had written, "Very cool today. Curt and I stacked rye." Following this is the last entry, in Mother's writing, "Blanche took sick."

The illness of the child was of the kind that today could be overcome by antibiotics, but in 1895 there was nothing Effie could do but cry, and the lightheartedness which she had exhibited earlier was gone. Eighteen days after Blanche died, Mother's mother died, with the same kind of fever. We say easily that time heals all, but in this we are wrong. In the nursing home in Indianola, where Mother spent the last nine years of her life, and where she died at the age of one hundred one and a half, the only photograph at which she looked regularly was that of Blanche. Though she lived nobly, the gaiety never returned, and the hurt was real, even seventy-three years later. After the tragic summer of 1895 Sam and Effie moved to the larger farm formerly owned by David Crew, and there three more children were born. My sister, Ethel, born in June 1897, now lives in retirement at Escondido, California, the widow of Loyal P. Thomas. I was born December 12, 1900, and my younger brother, Clare, now a physician in Indianola, was born December 15, 1906.

Of living children, grandchildren, great-grandchildren, and great-great-grandchildren of Sam and Effie there are now fifty. Not all are Quakers today, but all of us value the heritage which, without a break, has continued for more than three hundred years. One part of this inheritance comes from Germany. Our mother's maternal grandfather, Henry Smith, grew up in the

Quaker community of Minden where a Quaker burial ground still exists. He spent his last years in Iowa as a large land owner, but returned to Germany for many visits. It was undoubtedly from this strain, rather than from the Crews of Virginia, that Mother inherited her remarkable vitality. When she was eighty-five, living alone in an apartment, Mother was sufficiently forward-looking to purchase a new rug and to insist upon a thirty-year guarantee! For forty years she wrote to me at least once and often twice each week, until her illness in October 1964, after which she was never able to write again. When almost eighty-eight she wrote, "I never miss a day to pray God to guide you in all your doings." In old age she traveled several times by train to California and other parts of the country. The stone above her grave says "Effie Trueblood, 1867–1969."

My sister remembers vividly how, when she was about five years old, Mother pointed out to her the view to the southwest. There was not yet a tree in that direction, but as far as they could see, there was wild hay and waving grain. Directly across from our house, on the Adamson place, there were a few young trees backed by two cottonwoods, and that was all. Beyond them there was nothing to obscure the softly rolling hills. Mother told how her own mother, nearly thirty years earlier, had valued their three-room house because it provided the only shade she had. Mother's mother, Lydia, suffered from migraine headaches and never ceased to be homesick for the Ohio Valley. She took her little girl on one occasion and traveled back to Ohio for a visit, completing her tiresome journey by boat on the Muskingum River. Lydia lived to see two of her grandchildren, but she did not live long enough to adjust to the hard life of the prairie.

Something of the rapidity of development is indicated by the fact that the scene described by my sister was already altered at the time of my earliest memories. When I first became conscious of my surroundings, the orchards were already well grown, all the land was fenced, and trees were visible on the horizon.

In short, I was never part of the pioneer experience, though my early years were not far removed from it. When I try to think what my grandparents and other pioneers accomplished in a few decades, I am filled with admiration.

My own parents, when I was a very small child, enlarged the original house which Grandfather Crew had built, so that we had four bedrooms, including a guest room, and many other comforts. When I was six, our family had its first telephone, and about the same time rural mail delivery began. We had many flowers, including roses, a white picket fence, two barns, and many kinds of fruit trees. One of my most vivid memories is that of the days when the whole family shared in the task of filling glass jars with the abundant cherries. Our parents provided us with a rope swing, a hammock, a play wagon, and much more, to make the life of children a good one. For travel we used a two-seated carriage, drawn by high-spirited horses, which Mother drove as well as Father did.

The life I remember in my early childhood was indeed a good one. Nearly every farmer owned the land which he tilled, and there were no class distinctions of any kind. All helped one another, particularly at harvesttime and in the butchering of hogs. There were four public buildings in our village, and they seemed to suffice. The four were the general store, the blacksmith shop, the schoolhouse, and the meetinghouse. The blacksmith shop was necessary because plowshares required sharpening, wagon tires required welding, and horses required shoeing. The general store provided dry groceries, cloth, and various utensils, and also served as the post office. Once each week Ben Randolph, the storekeeper, went to the railroad six miles away and brought back a wagonload of merchandise. On rare occasions we drove sixteen miles to either Indianola or Knoxville, each a county seat, to take care of legal matters or to make major purchases.

The functions of the schoolhouse and the meetinghouse were

obvious. At the latter the pioneers gathered each Thursday morning as faithfully as they did on Sunday morning, whatever the sacrifice. Each housewife preserved hundreds of jars of fruit in the summer, and every farm had a smokehouse in which meat was cured. The fact that the nearest physician was six miles away was no real handicap, since we seldom needed his services. My mother never used the term midwife, but that is what she was for scores of her neighbors. At harvesttime she worked right along with Father in the fields and always milked the cows when he was detained elsewhere. By the winter of 1910, when we moved, all the farms, having been developed for forty years, had attained a high state of cultivation.

The one-room school was a good place for education to start. At the age of five and a half, when my schooling began, I was impressed with the knowledge of the big children whose recitations I could hear, and the motivation to emulate them was tremendous. I believe that we learned faster by not having been divided into grades. We came along early enough to use McGuffey's speller, priding ourselves on near perfection in that important discipline. Each teacher whom I remember was a dedicated woman who boarded in one of the nearby homes. Since our house was only a mile and a half from the school, my sister and I walked each way even in severe weather, taking turns in carrying the lunch pail.

The church life was of course dominant. A few miles to the south there were German Catholics, while a few miles to the east were Lutherans, but all of our close neighbors were Quakers, nearly every family having come from either Ohio or Indiana, and most of them stemming earlier from North Carolina. Four of the early families were Truebloods from Blue River, Indiana. The visiting ministers were often our guests, who contributed greatly to our contact with the outside world.

The excellence of our life at Waveland never dawned upon me until, as an adult, I first read the novels of Willa Cather, particularly *O Pioneers!* and *My Antonia,* and realized that the life in which I grew up was not essentially different from that in Nebraska about which Miss Cather had written so appealingly. No one had ever found Nebraska beautiful until Willa Cather wrote about it, because the others were too close to the struggle to realize the wonder of the drama in which they participated. Now, as I go back to the undulating land of southern Iowa, I admire what I see. I try to think how this fertile land looked when it was entirely devoid of human habitation. I know something of how hard the lives of the pioneers were, especially when I see the graves of five little boys belonging to one family. I am glad that in my childhood my own life overlapped the lives of really courageous people.

Good as our life was, in 1909 my parents began to sense an important problem. How could their children receive an education suitable to the new age into which they were moving? Ackworth Academy was about to close its doors, and daily travel to the nearest high school, six miles away, was out of the question. Accordingly, my parents sold the beautiful farm on which they had worked so hard and, at considerable financial sacrifice, purchased a farm near Indianola, where the schools were much admired. I can never express adequately my gratitude to my parents for this decision. Our new farm was smaller and more expensive, and it was necessary, furthermore, to build a new house.

I entered Indianola High School when I was twelve years old and graduated when I was sixteen. It is difficult for people today to understand the excellence of such a school. Because Simpson College was located in Indianola, O. E. Smith, the principal of the high school, was able to secure choice recent graduates as teachers, and he chose with remarkable skill. In four years I had first-class instruction in Latin, algebra, ancient history, English literature, physics, and even economics. When I was fifteen, Mother employed the college instructor in speech, who became my coach. I had never heard of such a thing, but Mother said it was as reasonable to pay for lessons in speech as for lessons in music. My tutor, a man well trained for his work, taught me how to regulate my voice and thus to be heard at a distance. Because of that fortunate connection, certain habits of speech soon became ingrained and remain to this day.

Though Indianola High School had athletic teams, I was never able to participate because my work on the farm after school was required for our family economy. All of every summer was of course spent in farm work. Sometimes I felt a touch of envy for those who were able to go on trips, but I knew I was needed. First, after the end of the school term, we cultivated the corn four times, twice each way. The cultivator which I used was for one row, and I walked behind it. As soon as the cultivation of the corn was completed, we normally harvested the small grain, both wheat and oats. Father drove the reaper, pulled by three big mares, and I did most of the placing of the bundles in what we called shocks. When my brother, six years younger, was old enough, he helped me in that labor. One year, 1915, the wheat produced forty bushels to the acre and Father could buy our first car, a Model T Ford. Since I was fourteen, I started at once to drive it, the State of Iowa requiring neither a driver's test nor a license. No road in our community was hard-surfaced, but each farmer accepted the responsibility of dragging about a mile of the dirt road, thus keeping it in fair shape.

The high point of summer was the threshing season. Since each farmer traded work with several others, there was no expense for labor. Our only financial outlay was our payment to the owner of the threshing machine and of the steam engine, which provided the power for the operation. The women helped each other, much as the men did, Mother's neighbors assisting her in the feeding of at least fifteen hungry workers. At every table during threshing there were both ham and fried chicken in abundance, as well as potatoes, various vegetables, and three

kinds of pie. In our little world everyone worked hard, everyone
was short of cash, and everyone ate bountifully. All of the people
rallied to help one another in times of sickness and other sorrow.
During Father's final illness, from March 1938 until his death
eight months later, the visitors who came to our farmhouse to
see him wrote their names. When I first saw the list I was really
amazed, for the names add up to several hundred. The impersonalism of the city was no part of our experience.

More and more it was the intellectual life which attracted me.
Father encouraged my hopes by speaking of his cousin, Thomas
Clarkson Trueblood, who had already achieved a reputation at
the University of Michigan, and for whom the new auditorium
at Ann Arbor is now named. In the summers I welcomed the
rainy days because they afforded me a chance to be with my
books and notebooks. My first experience of seeing my words in
print came in the summer of 1916 when the county newspaper
announced a contest, with essays on the significance of the
Declaration of Independence. I still remember working out the
sentences of my essay while I churned the butter. When to my
surprise I received first prize, ink seemed already to be in my
blood.

With the decline of the railroads it is hard for the new generation to know what the railroads meant to us sixty years ago.
Besides the Rock Island from the north, there was the Burlington from the south, running through Ackworth and Milo, and
connecting with the main line at Chariton. Every morning as
we were finishing our chores, we could hear the Burlington
whistle, and a little later we watched the Rock Island start to Des
Moines with its load of people. At night, long after we were in
bed, we could hear the whistle of the arriving midnight train.
Thus the trains were my timepiece before I owned a watch. As
we worked in the field, the arrival of the eleven-thirty train on
the Rock Island meant that we could stop for the morning, take
the horses to the barn for their feed and water, and enjoy lunch

ourselves. Because the horses needed a little rest, I could sometimes lie on the grass of our front lawn for a short while after
lunch, usually making plans for a future of which I could never
be wholly sure.

Chiefly because of Principal Smith, religious life in Indianola
High School was strong and pervasive. We had an active
Y.M.C.A., and in my senior year I was a member of the gospel
team. I don't suppose that anything which my teammates and
I had to say was worth the time of the listeners, but they
probably wanted to encourage us. I attended what was called an
"Older Boys Conference" at Grinnell, which was the farthest
from home I had ever been. The strongest single religious influence was that of the Christian Endeavor Society in the local
Friends Church. I signed the pledge to take some part, other
than singing, in every meeting of the Society, and also to engage
daily in both Bible reading and prayer. Honoring my signature,
I kept the promise, thus early learning something of the power
released by the voluntary acceptance of discipline. Years later,
when I began to dream of a new redemptive society, to be called
Yokefellows, my experience when I was fifteen and sixteen was
influential.

At the time of our settling in the Indianola community, in the
spring of 1910, there were several accessions to the local Friends
Church. Four or five new families, each with small children,
became both our neighbors and our close friends. Chief among
them were the Watlands, who on both sides were of Norwegian
ancestry. Mrs. Watland's father, John Frederic Hanson, had
sprung from the once thriving Quaker settlement at Stavanger,
Norway. Almost from the first, the Watlands and the Truebloods were the best of friends, celebrating both Thanksgiving
and Christmas alternately at each other's houses. Before transferring to schools in town, my sister and I had one year in a
country one-room school where the Watland children were likewise enrolled, and where the chief competition was between the

Friends and the non-Friends. Most of the Friends of Indianola were descendants of North Carolina families, just as we were. Characteristic names were Tomlinson, Honeycut, Hadley, Newlin, Haworth, Hiatt, and Frasier. Much later, when in my first teaching position I lived in North Carolina and encountered all of those names regularly, they seemed familiar because of my Iowa boyhood. It was remarkable how in spite of migration the heritage was maintained.

At first, on each Fourth of July, we went back to Milo where the celebration must have been one of the best anywhere. Always there was a speech, to which I never listened, and also a band, which I enjoyed. At noon each cluster of families sat on the grass, while the mothers brought out the piles of golden fried chicken and all that went with it. Ice cream we could purchase at stands, watching our money carefully to make it last all day. Father always gave each of us fifty cents. Those who had not spent too much otherwise could buy a ride in one of the new automobiles, going out to the cemetery and back for twenty-five cents. In later years our parents, deciding not to drive so far, celebrated Independence Day with a neighborhood picnic in Watlands' woods where the food was of course equally good, but unfortunately there was no band.

At the end of each summer came the State Fair at Des Moines. Both the Burlington and the Rock Island railroads ran special trains to accommodate the crowds which assembled each day, but the true State Fair attenders stayed for a solid week, camping on the grounds. To my boyish mind the Iowa State Fair was full of wonder. I liked especially the beautiful draft horses, Percheron, Clydesdale, Belgian, etc. We had begun to raise a few prize colts ourselves, and I was glad to observe what the professionals could do. The exhibits of handiwork, fruit, and baking were so numerous that a person could easily spend a week going slowly from building to building, without duplication. In the afternoons there was horse racing, and always there was the doubtful attraction of the midway, with its variety of booths, ferris wheels, and merry-go-rounds. When we took the late train back to Indianola we were very tired, but we inhabited a larger world because of our day at the fair.

Being only sixteen years old when I finished high school, I decided to omit formal education for a year. Though there was never any question whether I would go to college, it seemed better to postpone the experience. For one thing, I was too young, and, for another, I needed to earn money, even though my high school record automatically gave a college scholarship. During the year I grew physically and earned a little. At harvest-time, because Father was able to spare me, I worked for a farmer six miles away, living with his family. Each day started at 6 a.m. and ended at 7 p.m. The hardest times were those when I was shoveling wheat, trying to keep up with men much larger and stronger than myself. The headache was terrible, but my pride would never let me slacken the pace. For that work I received room and board and $37.50 a month, all of which was saved for college expenses.

During the winter of 1918, when I had abundant time to read on my own, Professor Edgar Stranahan of Penn College came to Indianola and gave a short course which I attended. From him I learned the best common sense that I have ever heard on how to prepare a speech or an essay. He advised starting with a large piece of paper and putting down as rapidly as possible, with no effort at order, every available idea on the subject under consideration. He said wisely that since the ideas, once listed, will soon begin to arrange themselves in some useful order, it is not necessary to begin with an outline. Ultimately, he said, the order is of paramount importance, but there must be content before there is form. The wisdom of this teaching has been verified countless times in my own experience.

Though World War I was still raging, I was too young to be drafted, and it was decided that I should enter Penn College in

September. The decision was a crucial one, since it led to many others, including that of my first marriage six years later. That my father, never having had the privilege of higher education himself, should care so much about it seems to me remarkable. As he sent me off in September 1918, he fitted me out handsomely, though he seldom spent any money on himself. Later, when I first read Thomas Carlyle's moving reminiscence of his father, I understood my own situation better. "With a noble faith," wrote Carlyle, "he launched me forth into a world which he himself had never been permitted to visit. Let me study to act worthily of him there."

2. Student

To be learning something is the greatest of pleasures, not only to the philosopher, but also to the rest of mankind.

Aristotle

After a disastrous fire in 1916 Penn College was moved to a new campus on the north edge of Oskaloosa, Iowa, where there was room for expansion. By the time I arrived in the autumn of 1918, three of the present buildings were already in use and something approaching an orderly academic life was possible. Because the war did not end until November of that year, the student population was still small. Women students lived in the fine new dormitory, now called Lewis Hall, but the men had to rent rooms in the homes of Oskaloosa citizens. Several dedicated women welcomed students as roomers and some as boarders. Male students, if they chose, ate with the young women in the dormitory dining room, and that I did for the first two years. Later I joined an eating club.

I felt keenly the need of easing the financial burden of my parents as much as I could, particularly since my sister was a senior in the same college. Fortunately, my high school scholarship canceled tuition and I was able to carry on two jobs. I received cash for mopping a local drugstore every day and earned my room rent by taking care of the coal furnace. The fact that I owned a bicycle made it possible for me to do my work at the downtown drugstore every morning between breakfast and my nine o'clock class. Naturally, I worked all of each summer on the farm without pay. During the influenza epidemic of 1918 when classes were dismissed, I was able to secure a job picking corn a few miles from the college, for which I was paid three cents a bushel. Thus, in a normal day, by working at top speed I could earn two dollars.

During my freshman year I had two academic experiences which left permanent marks upon my life. The first was my start on the Greek language. With Dr. William E. Berry as our teacher and with only five of us in the class, the incentive to learn was very strong, and certainly there was no chance to escape responsibility. In spite of having already studied Latin for four years, Greek was so difficult for me that I had to adopt the practice of waking every morning at five o'clock to work on it until breakfast time. Already I realized that I was a morning person, and though I had not yet heard the maxim, "Never use prime time for second-rate tasks," I knew that I needed to use the time of my greatest intellectual energy for whatever was most difficult. Greek is not a popular subject of study today, and only a minority will undertake it, but I am glad to testify to what it did for me as I began my college education. Its most lasting effect, I believe, was in the field of English grammar.

The second experience which affected me deeply was my course in English composition taught by a highly dedicated woman, Anna Eves. Every Monday for nine months I handed Miss Eves an essay of six hundred words. When I think of the fortitude of that good woman, who faced every week that recurring pile of essays, I am amazed that she could do it. She took seriously everything we wrote, and sought to help us to write better. I now know that this is the only way in which literary production can be taught. The essence of the undertaking is the steadiness and persistence involved in the operation. People learn to write by writing, by writing repeatedly, and by accepting the criticism of those who are both caring and demanding. The regularity of the requirement is essential. If I had been allowed to write only when I felt like it, I should have produced very little. Much of what I wrote was poor, but fortunately my tutor told me wherein it was poor.

Because the military draft ended with the end of the war, and because that occurred one month before my eighteenth birthday, I was never drafted. Those who had been soldiers came back to college so speedily that, beginning with my sophomore year, the college population was visibly increased. Among those who came back were young men who had served with the Friends Reconstruction Unit in France, and from them I learned something about life in Europe. By the autumn of 1919 there was a prospect of good intercollegiate football with a coach who had been a varsity player at Notre Dame. Not having the same reason for not participating in sports which I had had in high school, I tried out for football and played in three seasons. I find it difficult to explain the precise value of intercollegiate football, but I know that it helped me immensely. The toughness of the discipline, the necessity of going on in spite of fatigue, and the comradeship with my teammates made a real difference in my life.

When the football season was over, we started our debating schedule, competing all winter with other colleges. I was on the debate team of Penn all four years and also participated in public speaking contests. As the representative of the college I shared in the State Extempore Speaking Contest in 1922 and was awarded first prize, with a gold medal. It was part of the merit of the college which I attended that clear expression was looked upon, not as an extra gloss, but as one reasonable mark of an educated person.

So far as I can remember, every professor at Penn College was a dedicated person. I do not know exactly what salaries were paid, but I know that they were low and that many of my teachers could have bettered themselves financially by serving elsewhere.

Though the number of books in the library was not large, I cherished my hours spent among them, and more and more I turned to the stacks where the volumes of philosophy were found. The only real competitor for my attention was the section devoted to literary criticism.

When I graduated in 1922, I had never been beyond the borders of the state of my birth, but I knew where I wanted to go when I could. First of all, I wanted to be in New England, and thither I went immediately after graduation on June 7. Having Forrest Comfort, a fellow graduate, as companion, and wishing my first long journey to be as educational as possible, the trip from Iowa to Rhode Island was made in stages. We took the night train from Des Moines to Chicago and spent most of the following day among the sights of Chicago, particularly visiting the museums. Then we went by railroad to Detroit where we took the night boat the length of Lake Erie, arriving at Buffalo in the morning and going at once to Niagara Falls. That night we went by New York Central train to Albany where we began the boat trip on the Hudson River by day. The last leg of the journey was by train to Providence and on to Woonsocket where I was to live. My plan was to serve the Friends Meeting of Woonsocket and to attend classes at Brown University three days a week. In Woonsocket I made enduring friendships, especially with Melita and Nellie Fisher at whose gracious home I lived and whose fellowship I still prize after fifty years.

The most wonderful feature of the summer of 1922 was that I had freedom to read books which I had not had time to read while still an undergraduate. Slowly I went through *Sartor Resartus*, thus having my first real encounter with the mind of Thomas Carlyle. Another book which I had time to read slowly was *The Philosophy of Loyalty* by Josiah Royce. I liked the unhurried pace so much that I have encouraged my own students to keep a list of books to enjoy someday when they are liberated from academic pressures. Life in Union Village, a suburb of Woonsocket, was strikingly dissimilar to my life in Iowa. The fact that a large part of the Woonsocket population was French speaking, and that street signs were in French, gave me the impression at times that I was actually in a foreign country. The many mills provided me with my first experience of an industrial culture.

I have always been glad that I could begin my graduate study at Brown, where long hours of uninterrupted study in the John Hay Library were highly productive. There, among other things, I had time to read nearly all of the works of Auguste Comte and soon saw the inadequacy of the Positive Philosophy. With no extracurricular interests and no time spent in courtship except for correspondence, I began in a modest way to pursue the life of scholarship. My first graduate seminar, which introduced me to a new approach to study, dealt with the problems presented by the Synoptic Gospels.

In February 1923 there occurred my most memorable experience at Brown. I received a note from W. P. Faunce, the distinguished president of the university, asking me to visit him in his office. To my surprise he offered me a position, with membership on the Brown faculty, teaching at the University of Shanghai as the representative of "Brown-in-China." Since I was only twenty-two years old, the offer was overwhelming. In college I had been associated with the Student Volunteer Movement and had attended, with eight thousand other students, the national conference of the movement at Des Moines in January 1920. Still inspired as I was by the words of John R. Mott, service in China seemed very appealing, but I was conscious of the inadequacy of my preparation. I wrote to Pauline Goodenow, asking her opinion and also asking whether she would accompany me as my wife should I go. She stayed up all night, trying to decide, and finally concluded that she was willing, but by that time I had become even more doubtful of my readiness for a move of such proportions. Accordingly, the offer was declined and we were not married until a year later.

One incident in my memorable interview with President Faunce has stayed in my mind, though I am sure it did not stay in his. While we were talking on the subject which was highly important for my career, I was shocked to see the great man suddenly stop speaking, take out a notebook, and write in it for three or four minutes, while I sat in silence. When he had finished writing, President Faunce again spoke to me, asking my pardon for his seeming discourtesy. Then he explained that ideas were his capital and that he had suddenly had an idea not connected with our immediate conversation. He went on to say that he had learned to put down ideas when they came because otherwise they might be lost forever. Far from being hurt, as he feared I might be, I was immensely grateful. With rare exceptions I have carried a notebook ever since and have learned that my ideas are not retained unless they are recorded.

Most of my second year of graduate study was spent at Hartford Theological Seminary, in Hartford, Connecticut, with trips back to Woonsocket every weekend. The chief enduring value of that year lay in the friendship of one man, Dr. Alexander Purdy, whom I came to love as well as to respect. Each Sunday afternoon Dr. Purdy, as he traveled from Providence to Hartford, picked me up at Union Village and drove me to our mutual destination. We were free to talk about anything that interested us, and I absorbed more than the teacher realized.

Another Hartford dividend was the beginning of my friendship with Thomas Kelly. Little could we know that thirteen years later he would be my successor in the philosophy department at Haverford College or that as editor of *The Friend* I would solicit articles from him, which would be published in book form after his untimely death. The book, *A Testament of Devotion*, which has been reprinted many times since its first appearance in 1941, is widely recognized as one of the few devotional masterpieces of our century.

Early in May 1924 I went to England for my first visit overseas in order to share, as a representative of American Young Friends, in the various activities by which the three hundredth anniversary of George Fox was marked, and to study, for the summer term, at Woodbrooke College in Birmingham. The fruits of the trip were many, including an affectionate contact with British Quakers which has been strengthened by nine subsequent visits of varying length. In my student experience I was influenced by two famous scholars, Dr. Rendel Harris and Dr. Herbert G. Wood. Rendel Harris was already a fabulous figure, partly because of his early academic success on the well-known team of scholars at Johns Hopkins University. For the first time in my life I observed a person who combined, with no apparent self-consciousness or even difficulty, the warm heart and the clear head. Like all who knew "the Doctor," as he was invariably called, I was aware of his meticulous Biblical scholarship which included discoveries in the Sinai Desert, but what struck me most was the great man's unabashed piety. I saw him drop to his knees and pray vocally with the simplicity of a little child. Though I realized that such an attractive combination is rare, I noted the important fact that it is possible.

Fifteen years later, when I was in Birmingham as a Fellow of Woodbrooke, Rendel Harris invited me to tea in his house. The date, as I easily verify by my journal, was Whitsunday, May 28, 1939. It was the last year of the good Doctor's life in that he died a few months after the start of the war, as the result of a bomb explosion. He sat with me in his garden, nearly blind, and spoke to me as "my dear boy." We talked of President Daniel C. Gilman, Professor Basil L. Gildersleeve, Sir William Osler, and other Hopkins greats. When I asked the secret of the intellectual renaissance at Hopkins in his time, he answered, "It was really very simple; we all attended each other's lectures." I agreed that it would tone a man up to have in his audience regular attenders of the character of Dr. Osler. Present-day academic experience would be improved if professors should lecture less frequently, attempting to reach a high standard on each occasion.

Shortly before I became his student, Herbert G. Wood had produced two remarkable articles for Peake's *Commentary on the Bible*, "The Life and Teaching of Jesus" and "Mark." It was thrilling to hear Professor Wood lecture, but it was even more so to watch him play tennis. I knew that I was acquiring models.

On my return from England at the end of August 1924 Pauline Goodenow and I were married and settled at once in Boston. I accepted the appointment as executive secretary of the Friends Meeting in Roxbury, partly because that gave us housing and a small salary which would enable me to pursue my studies in Harvard Divinity School. There were many reasons for my transfer to Harvard, but the crucial factor was the appeal of a person. I wanted to study where I could be associated with Willard L. Sperry.

By the time of my arrival at Harvard Willard L. Sperry was dean of the Divinity School and also dean of the Chapel. From the beginning he took a close personal interest in me and finally became my tutor, criticizing my papers in a regular and meticulous fashion. Later it pleased me greatly when Dean Sperry asked me to be acting dean of the Chapel at Harvard for the summer of 1935 and acting professor of the Philosophy of Religion in the autumn of 1944. His greatest academic assistance, so far as I was concerned, arose from our mutual examination of the Christian classics of devotion and the long poems of William Wordsworth. In frequent private meetings Dean Sperry urged me to soak myself in the great models, apart from which advice I might not have begun my contact with the works of Dr. Samuel Johnson. Thus I became involved in what Whitehead called "the habitual vision of greatness." Others to whom Dean Sperry introduced me as masters of style were William Hazlitt and Olive Schreiner.

All of the courses at the Divinity School were well taught by men whose scholarship was unquestioned. The most eminent was George Foot Moore, from whom I heard lectures in his field of greatest competence, the history of religions. By good fortune he was the chairman of my oral examiners when I qualified for my Harvard degree. The other professors were so afraid of Moore and of his possible attack, if he considered any questions unfair, that they were uniformly kind to me. Actually most of the questions were asked by Professor Moore himself.

It was a matter of pride with me that while I was a student at Harvard Divinity School I never saw any grades. Since the grades were not mailed to us, it was necessary for anyone who wished to see them to go in person to an office in the Yard. I did not go because I felt that ours was a mature operation and that the only real rewards were those involved in personal growth. Even the Harvard preaching prize was not very important except that it produced a little money.

When I enrolled at Harvard I began at once the practice of putting my lecture notes into bound notebooks, easily placed on a shelf. Consequently, I have a full record of every course, each in a separate volume, without the confusion of loose leaves. My practice was to write nothing but complete sentences, recasting whatever was said into a form which seemed to me suitable for use on later occasions. The discipline of forcing myself to consolidate about three sentences into one, making the reasoning as continuous as possible, was one which helped me. I had already discovered that there is no probability of impression without expression, and the act of forcing myself to express thoughts in words which were partly my own became increasingly valuable.

Each morning I took the elevated train from Dudley Station into the heart of Boston where I changed to the Cambridge subway, emerging in Harvard Square. I used the travel time for light reading, going straight through *Pickwick Papers* in that fashion. The walk through the Yard and up Divinity Avenue always reminded me of others who had walked that way. In the old Chapel of Divinity Hall I tried to imagine Ralph Waldo Emerson as he delivered there one of his most famous addresses. I felt from the first that I belonged, and learned that graduation from a small college in Iowa was no handicap whatever. After all, nearly everyone had come from somewhere. Dean Sperry was himself a product of a college like mine, Olivet in Michigan, from which he had gone on to be a Rhodes Scholar in Oxford. So far as I can remember, no inquiry about origins was ever made. In Cambridge I had my first view of Ivy League football and in Boston my first experience of high-class music in Symphony Hall. I enjoyed visiting the old bookstores, especially those in the Park Street area. My education was indeed many-sided!

The fact that a student in the Divinity School could, without added expense, pursue courses in any school or department of the entire university seemed to me then, and seems to me now, a distinct advantage. Accordingly, I determined to use the opportunity thus provided. Five such courses were extremely valuable in my development.

The first was a course in the history of Gothic architecture taught by the dean of the School of Architecture. I had already seen and admired some of the famous English cathedrals, and I was eager for a deeper understanding of what the anonymous builders of the Middle Ages were trying to accomplish. I did not, of course, lay claim to any ability in drawing, but I found the principles of construction appealing.

My second course was one of the most admired in the entire university, Bliss Perry's course on the life and thought of

Thomas Carlyle. There I came into personal contact with the most competent teacher I had met up to that time. We read all of the major works of Carlyle, wrote papers on them, and listened to two lectures a week. The fact that there were two hundred forty of us in the class created no problem at all. A man of Professor Perry's ability could lecture to many as capably as to a few. We applauded the teacher at the end of every lecture because each was a masterpiece. Realizing more than before that teaching can be a very great art, I determined to emulate Perry's standard if I could. When he entertained me in his home, the atmosphere proved to be warm and friendly.

My third course, already mentioned in the preface to this book, was devoted to seventeenth-century religious prose. I had known that the seventeenth century was a flowering time spiritually, though I had not yet encountered Whitehead's appealing phrase, "The century of genius," but apart from this course I could not have felt the powerful impact of so many first-rate minds. To live for weeks with the thoughtful expressions of John Donne, John Bunyan, John Milton, Richard Baxter, Jeremy Taylor, Thomas Traherne, and Robert Barclay was something truly memorable. Without this experience I doubt if Barclay would have attracted me as he later did.

A fourth course of enduring value was that called poetics, taught by a visiting scholar from England, Professor Oliver Elton. The fact that his surname was the same as my Christian name drew us together personally, but it was the forcefulness of the pioneers of literary criticism that made the most difference in my thinking. Though, under Dr. Berry at Penn College, I had already read the plays of Sophocles, Aeschylus, and Euripides, that was my first opportunity to study *The Poetics of Aristotle*. The work and influence of Longinus had been, until that time, wholly unknown to me. Professor Elton understood the Greek thinkers, but he understood the modern ones equally well. The ideas of Sidney, Burke, Wordsworth, Coleridge, and many more came to me with a freshness that was revealing. Conceivably, I could have read all of them on my own, but the likelihood that I would ever have done so is slight. Partly because, through Dean Sperry's encouragement, I had some idea of becoming a professional writer, I saw that Professor Elton's teaching was highly pertinent to my career.

The fifth nontheological course was the seminar in Hegel taught by Professor William Ernest Hocking. That was the only course I followed in the year 1926-1927 when I remained in Cambridge after taking my Harvard degree. At the same time I was spending long unhurried hours in Emerson Hall reading, on my own, right through the *Dialogues* of Plato. That particular combination was fruitful for my intellectual growth. The Hocking seminar met in the dining room of the professor's house near the University Club, providing a setting unknown to me earlier. We were expected to be able to read Hegel without translation from the German, and that turned out to be the most strenuous work I had ever undertaken, for *The Phenomenology of Mind* is hard enough even when put into English. Glad as I was to try to understand the philosophy of Hegel, I was even more so to be in regular contact with such a truly civilized person as my instructor turned out to be.

One interesting episode of the extra year in Cambridge was the burglarizing of our apartment on Massachusetts Avenue. One night, when dinner was completed, I went to our bedroom to find that a window was wide open. Our winter coats, some of Pauline's dresses, and even her wedding ring were gone. She had removed the ring that afternoon for the first time since our marriage because she had burned a finger. What frightened us most was that our first child, Martin, was asleep in the apartment, but fortunately he was not harmed. The next night the apartment of Herbert Hoover, Jr., was likewise burglarized, again with a young child unharmed. A burglar who was caught in a similar crime the following night confessed to burglarizing both of us. That led to our first acquaintance with the Hoovers, whom we came to know better in later years, particularly in connection with former President Hoover's funeral in 1964. We often spoke of the strange beginning of our friendship. When Herbert Hoover, Jr., died in Pasadena in the summer of 1969, I conducted his memorial service.

So far as my student experience was concerned, the three-year period, 1927-1930, was an interim one, during which I did my first teaching. Though any teacher who tries to be worthy of his calling is always a student, my three years at Guilford College, North Carolina, were such that futher formal education had to be postponed. In January 1930 came the crucial decision to seek the Doctor of Philosophy degree. The depression had begun two months earlier and our second son, Arnold, had just been born. During the second semester at Guilford all salaries were severely reduced in an effort to balance a depression budget. That seemed a strange time to rock the boat, but I was twenty-nine years old and realized that if I were ever to carry on advanced work in philosophy, I dare not wait.

Pauline kept telling me jokingly that a man who was a really good philosopher and a good teacher did not need the Ph.D. because he could operate very well without it. She pointed out that Socrates had no degree. When I answered that I doubted if I were strong enough to go against the current academic stream, she bravely agreed to work with me, whatever my decision. Accordingly, I called on the president of the college, handing him my resignation to take effect in June 1930.

By a remarkable combination of circumstances it became possible for our little family to establish ourselves in Baltimore in September 1930. Fortunately, or providentially, there was offered me by Baltimore Friends a salaried position with the understanding that I could, while serving the Yearly Meeting, engage in graduate studies at Johns Hopkins University, with an office in Homewood Meetinghouse across the street from the university campus. I took time to organize a weekly luncheon club of undergraduates, specifically inviting the men who on registration had listed themselves as agnostics. The club, which lasted three years, we called "The How to Be Religious Though Intelligent on Wednesday Club."

From the first my one and only mentor at Johns Hopkins University was Professor Arthur O. Lovejoy, then one of the most respected philosophers of America, operating at the height of his powers. A former president of the American Philosophical Association, he had, seven years earlier, founded "The History of Ideas Club" and was deeply involved in his studies of the Great Chain of Being and Nature as a Norm. When I became associated with this remarkable man, he was fifty-seven years old.

Lovejoy's seminars became famous. Long familiar with youthful ignorance and arrogance, he responded with the deftness of a true professional. Every member of a seminar, so far as I can remember, soon understood that the man with short gray hair had no intention of tolerating ambiguity. If anyone claimed to be a pragmatist, he had to be prepared to explain to which of the known forms of pragmatism he referred. "With his eyes upon you," wrote a student in retrospect, "you would weigh your words twice before uttering them. His presence discouraged laxity of thought, intellectual bravado, and facile talking."

The dignity of the seminar setting was heightened for me by the fact that President Gilman's bust was visible. Lovejoy sat at the end of the big table, and always encouraged participation as he developed his theme, but the more mature the students became, the more they were in awe of their teacher. The awesomeness of Lovejoy was, however, only one side of his character. Another side was his genuine interest in his students. One of them wrote, "I do not mean that I was afraid of him. He was more than approachable and always willing to assist his students in every way. Because he seemed to me Zeus on Olympus, it was always a surprise to learn how very human he really was." I do not think I was afraid of him either; I simply wanted to do my best in his presence and to deserve his approbation.

The common enemies of the philosophy department were vagueness, ambiguity, equivocation, and confusion. In one sense the constant topic of all the teaching was the title made famous years earlier at Hopkins by C. S. Peirce, "How to Make Our Ideas Clear." Under Lovejoy's tuition, clarity became my professional goal, whether in written or spoken communication. I realized that there is little chance of making clear to others what is not clear to ourselves.

Never married, Lovejoy seemed to be the extreme scholastic, but he was fond of children and he engaged in a variety of practical tasks devoted to human welfare. It was always to philosophy, however, that he was supremely devoted. From the beginning he taught me to try to disprove every hypothesis I proposed. The essence of his own vision is caught in the words of his eminent colleague, Professor George Boas, who said, in Lovejoy's terms, "Philosophy, like science, is not determined by psychological causes but by evidence and logical consistency." It was no accident that during the twenty-two years that I taught, after I ceased to be Lovejoy's student, I always tried to make logic the central discipline. The basic question concerning any dictum, I soon saw, is not why someone believes it, but whether it is objectively true. Trying always to be a Christian, I learned from both Hocking and Lovejoy that if Christianity is not true it is an evil. It is not enough for a conviction to be comforting or to satisfy some psychological need.

During my second year at Johns Hopkins I wrote essays, submitting them to Professor Lovejoy, and later discussing them with him in his house at 827 Park Avenue. He seemed to take a special interest in me when he learned that I was a Quaker. Having served at the university since 1910, he remembered the time when many of the board of trustees were Quakers and was aware, of course, that Mr. Hopkins was one himself. Once

Professor Lovejoy came to the Homewood Meetinghouse to listen to Professor Rufus M. Jones during a session of Baltimore Yearly Meeting.

My close association with one of the most famous teachers of our generation lasted four years. For three of these we lived in Baltimore, but for the fourth we lived in Pennsylvania, whither I had gone to teach at Haverford College. During my first year of teaching at Haverford I wrote one chapter a month on my doctoral dissertation, traveling to Baltimore at the end of each month to confer with Professor Lovejoy. Though he was increasingly kind to me, he never relaxed his standards, and every line had to be justified. Near the end, in May 1934, he gave a dinner for two of us after we had defended our dissertations. The dinner was a dignified affair, served with meticulous care and with recognized protocol in regard to speeches. Lovejoy realized that civilization is fragile and that it will be lost unless standards are observed. One example of his sense of propriety concerned tobacco. Though he was himself a smoker in private life, he would have evicted any student who undertook to smoke in one of the famous seminars.

Knowing that I had a variety of responsibilities, Professor Lovejoy feared that I might scatter my energies too much. At one of our private conferences he said, "Don't ever depart from the practice of philosophy." When I took the position in the philosophy department at Haverford, he was pleased because he thought that my new responsibilities would tend to keep me from straying.

The opportunities open to a student at Johns Hopkins during the depression were rich and varied. Our department brought to the campus a succession of distinguished visitors, among the most stimulating being the brilliant English logician, Susan Stebbing, by whom all of the professors, including Professor Lovejoy himself, seemed to be awed. If she did nothing else, she helped, by demonstration, to show the untenability of the supposition that logical skill is a male monopoly. John Dewey gave a set of lectures, but I found him surprisingly dull. The most exciting of the visiting lecturers was T. S. Eliot, who lectured in a fascinating manner on "The Metaphysical Poets." The conjunction of piety and tough intelligence, represented in such a man of genius, tended to raise the standards of at least one who heard him.

The examinations in both German and French were, I knew, difficult ones. I therefore tried to find a way to speed up my preparation for them. A really useful procedure was that of reading the four Gospels in both German and French translations. Being already familiar with most of the passages in English, I thus avoided the necessity of a constant use of dictionaries and consequently increased my speed in comprehension. Whoever suggested that method did me a genuine service.

My chief work as a graduate student was done in a cubicle assigned to me among the library stacks of Gilman Hall. There I could collect books at my own discretion without signing them out or regularly returning them to the various shelves. I occupied that particular cubicle for three years. Slowly but joyfully as I studied, I began to see where I believed my major emphasis should be placed. For a while I thought of writing on the moral philosophy of Albert Schweitzer, and even received the famous doctor's permission in a letter written from Lambarene, West Africa. But it later became evident to me that great as Schweitzer was as a person, his philosophy was not of sufficient substance.

More and more I concentrated upon what some had begun to call "philosophical anthropology." I came to believe that the single most important fact which we know about our universe is that, at one point at least, it is the home of *persons*. The more I thought, the better I liked the idea because, far from being merely speculative as so many ideas are, it is strictly empirical. I realized that the question of human uniqueness has been central to the thinking of philosophers in all ages. I meditated long upon the phenomenon, not only of consciousness, but of self-consciousness. Professor Lovejoy encouraged me, for he also turned again and again to that phenomenon. One of his most profound lectures, given at Swarthmore College in 1941, was entitled "The Self-Appraisal of Man," while another was called "The Desires of the Self-Conscious Animal." The opening sentence in the Swarthmore College lectures was, "The maxim that the knowledge man needs most is knowledge of himself was an article of the religious creed of the Greeks at least two and a half millennia ago." I found myself turning not only to Socrates, but to the Psalmist with his haunting question, "What is man that thou art mindful of him?" Those are the words inscribed on the wall of Emerson Hall at Harvard. It was Lovejoy's central conviction that, since thinking can make a difference in the course of events, man is a being who needs to learn to think well. Philosophy is, above all, thinking about thinking!

As any careful reader of my philosophical books will quickly note, the theme of my Hopkins dissertation has continued to attract me. *General Philosophy,* intended to be my most thorough approach to metaphysics and epistemology, includes a chapter, "Man and Animal." In that chapter is a sentence from a Scottish philosopher which still seems to me to be profoundly true: "The breach between ethical man and pre-human nature constitutes without exception the most important fact which the universe has to show." That does not mean that man is naturally good—far from it. Our hope lies, not in any natural goodness, as some eighteenth-century philosophers erroneously supposed, but rather in the self-consciousness which makes it possible for persons to examine what they do and sometimes, in consequence, to change.

The fact of self-consciousness, which we often take for granted, is best seen if it is approached with wonder and is recognized, accordingly, as a revelation of the nature of basic reality. I have many reasons for believing that God, the Infinite Person, exists, and is not merely a projection of our hopes, but my most compelling reason, after years of thinking on the subject, is the emergence of self-conscious beings at the one point in the universe that we know fairly well. It is increasingly obvious to me that self-consciousness cannot be the product of unconsciousness! Since I first heard the aphorism, I have believed, with some of the early Greeks, that nothing comes from nothing.

Only in retrospect have I been able to see that I was very fortunate in my total student experience, and that one of my blessings is that of a good education. My student life, from my first day in country school to the conferring of my Hopkins degree, amounting to nearly twenty-eight years, is really one of the longest chapters of my life. But of course it never really ended. I hope to remain a student as long as I live.

3. Teacher

And gladly wolde he learne, and gladly teche.
Chaucer

In the months which followed my graduation from the Divinity School there were several invitations to engage in pastoral work. On March 3, 1927, I met in friendly conference with Bishop Charles L. Slattery who stressed the comprehensive character of the Episcopal Church and assured me of a warm welcome if I were to turn in its direction. When I reported that to my wife, she expressed the firm conviction that I ought to remain a Quaker, not because Friends had a monopoly on the truth, but because with that as my base I could be more effective in the world. As we talked, I found that I fully agreed, and the decision thus made is one which I have never regretted. My being a Quaker has opened more doors than it has closed.

There remained the practical question of which particular role to follow. Then in April 1927 there arrived a letter which helped to determine the course of our lives. Because of some articles of mine which had been published, Dr. Raymond Binford of Guilford College had already asked me to give the Bac-

calaureate Address at the commencement of 1926. It was almost
a year later that he wrote, inviting me to inaugurate Guilford's
first department of philosophy. Since I had never taught anywhere and was only twenty-six years old, the proposal was fright-
ening, but it was also attractive. Some assistance came when
Pauline said she thought teaching was my forte, and we decided
to move from New England to the South. Though we stayed
only three years, the move was an auspicious one.

Guilford College, when we arrived in September 1927, was in
the country, six miles out the Friendly Road from Greensboro.
Today the population has grown so much that the Guilford
campus is actually in the city. Having been founded by North
Carolina Quakers in 1837, the college was a well-respected institution with about four hundred students equally divided between women and men. We were assigned the use of a small
house on the wooded campus close enough to the dormitories
to bring us into contact with the students at all times. As dean
of men I had an office in one of the dormitories and found it
possible to know by name nearly all of the men as well as some
of the women. Martin, who was two years old, soon learned to
wander about the campus and became a welcome visitor in
student rooms.

I tried to combine lectures and seminars, the latter being
devoted to the study of major philosophical works. Because
reprints were rather inexpensive, it was reasonable to expect
even the students who were on low budgets to purchase the
classics, which they might keep all of their lives as cherished
possessions. One enterprise which provided me much satisfaction was my first course in Christian Classics, modeled to some
extent on that taught by Dean Sperry at Harvard. I soon found
that it was comparatively easy to interest students in the works
of Augustine, à Kempis, and Pascal because the thoughts of
these men are not limited to their time. My own mind grew as
I attempted my first teaching, some of the books which I

analyzed being then read by me for the first time.

Life at Guilford was pleasant in numerous ways. We reveled in the beautiful climate of the Piedmont, became acquainted with the surrounding towns, and on clear days looked at the beginning of the mountains to the northwest. On Sunday evenings the living room of our campus house was filled with forty or more students in what we laughingly called the Heretics Club because there were no limits to what could be discussed without embarrassment. The difference in age between us and the students was actually not great, though that fact was not evident at the time. When I meet those same people now, the five or six years' difference seems to have faded, and we feel like contemporaries. At the beginning of the football season I put on a uniform and practiced with the players, which had the double effect of helping me to keep physically fit and becoming acquainted with more students. Also there was a good opportunity to play tennis, sometimes with fellow instructors, but chiefly with students.

Leaving Guilford College in the summer of 1930, I was as loyal to the institution as when I joined it. It had given me a magnificent opportunity to learn to teach. We were far from affluent, my salary never rising above $2,700 a year. By my leaving, a place was made for Clyde Milner who, after a brief period of teaching, was elected president of the college and served with great distinction in that capacity for more than thirty years.

My second experience of college teaching was, as we have seen, at Haverford, a Quaker college for men located on Philadelphia's Main Line. Because Professor Douglas Steere was granted a leave of absence in the academic year 1933-1934, and also because that was the last year of teaching for Professor Rufus M. Jones, the opening in the philosophy department was a permanent one. Rufus Jones wrote to me, telling about the opening and asking me to pay a visit to Haverford in order to discuss the possibility. Of course I went with alacrity, attended the "Fifth Day Meeting" in the Haverford meetinghouse, which was then required of all students, and enjoyed a friendly conference with William W. Comfort, president of the college. I knew that the work would be difficult, since it would be necessary to teach courses of which I had had no previous experience, and also to finish my Hopkins dissertation at the same time, but the prospects were alluring, chiefly because Haverford standards were high. With our two little boys we moved to Haverford in September 1933 and began a rewarding three-year period. Since my beginning annual salary was only $3,300, it was still necessary to be very careful with expenditures. There was no possibility of our owning a car, but we hardly missed one because transportation on the Paoli Local into Philadelphia was excellent and the big trains, all of which stopped for passengers at Paoli, were at the peak of their performance.

The most enjoyable classes for which I was solely responsible at Haverford were Introduction to Philosophy, and Logic, but the joint seminar with Dr. Jones was on an entirely different level. Dr. Jones lived in an old house facing the cricket field. In the afternoons he sat on his porch, in a rocking chair, watching the students play and chatting with passers-by. He could afford to relax because his work for the day had been done. By inflexible rule he went to bed every night at ten o'clock and rose early the next morning, refreshed and alert. All of his creative work was done in the early morning hours, when he disciplined himself against interruption. Indeed, he would not even go to the college post office to collect his mail until his assigned work was accomplished, for he well knew how diverting letters can be. Though he subscribed to a daily newspaper, he allotted little time to it and often read it while standing. When I became his junior colleague, he was seventy and I was thirty-two.

Our joint seminar, which met in Dr. Jones' upstairs study, was attended by seniors concentrating in philosophy. The first semester, taught by Dr. Jones, dealt with Kant, while the second semester, which I taught, dealt with Hegel. It was my chance to profit by what I had learned from William Ernest Hocking in his house at Cambridge. Best of all, I had a splendid opportunity to watch Dr. Jones' technique and to try to understand the secret of his power. Part of it, I soon saw, was his authentic friendliness. He really cared about the senior men, and they could not fail to know that. They are mature men now, and they may not remember much of the *Critique of Pure Reason*, but they can never forget Rufus Jones.

Another part of my teaching duty during my first year at Haverford College was that of assisting Dr. Jones in his famous class in ethics. Since it was my duty to read all of the papers, I necessarily attended all of the lectures. The course was required of every senior and was intended as a kind of capstone of the college studies. It was valuable, not primarily in its analysis of moral philosophy, but in its reflections on human life in general, from the point of view of one wise man who seemed much as Socrates must have seemed at the end of his career. His teaching reminded me of the possibly apocryphal answer of Professor Whitehead to a student who inquired what courses he offered: "I have three courses," he is reported to have said, "Whitehead I, Whitehead II, and Whitehead III." Everyone at Haverford knew in late May 1934 that a particular age was coming to an end. Though the master teacher lived on for fourteen more years, he never taught again. Now, when I visit the burial ground by the Haverford meetinghouse, I am deeply moved as I look at the small stone which records nothing of his degrees, books, or honors, but says, in magnificent simplicity, "Rufus M. Jones, 1863–1948." He was a man of whom it could truly be said, as Thomas Carlyle said of his wife, Jane, that he "had the gift of calling forth the best qualities that were in people."

Though we left Haverford at the end of three years of teaching, the friendship with the Jones family continued in an intimate fashion. When our daughter was born, we named her Elizabeth for Mrs. Jones, and I was able to be of some help after Rufus Jones died.

The greatest single advance in my teaching career during my Haverford chapter came in the field of logic. I soon became convinced that the study of logic, including scientific method, is one of the most important steps in the development of trained minds. I saw that logical thinking can apply to every aspect of experience, including religion. I tried to teach my students to face every problem by careful analysis, by the construction of hypotheses which exhaust the logical possibilities, and by the elimination of all hypotheses except one. It was not by accident, therefore, that my first serious academic work in religion was entitled *The Logic of Belief.* What I learned by my teaching of logic at Haverford College had enduring effects in my subsequent teaching at both Stanford University and Earlham College.

Teaching at Haverford brought many means of growth not limited to the campus. Connections with the neighboring institutions, Bryn Mawr and Swarthmore, were uniformly helpful. I attended the philosophical club of the area, which included teachers from Pennsylvania, Lehigh, and Lafayette universities, as well as the three colleges founded by Friends. Especially valuable to me were papers by Brand Blanchard, then of Swarthmore, and Paul Weiss, then of Bryn Mawr, my friendship with those thinkers continuing after both of them had transferred to Yale. Some of the key chapters of Dr. Blanchard's book, *The Nature of Thought,* which was not published until 1940, were read to us in 1935. It was a fine experience to observe the genesis of a distinguished philosophical work.

In the autumn of 1934 Douglas Steere returned from his year in Europe and the two of us taught all of the philosophy courses. The summer of 1935 our family spent in Cambridge, occupying the house of Henry J. Cadbury, Hollis Professor of Divinity at

Harvard. It pleased me that my former dean, Willard L. Sperry, invited me to take his place while he was in England. Contacts made in Cambridge with some students that summer have remained until this day, but the most important aspect of my first Harvard appointment lay in the development to which it led, rather than in itself. It was because of the interim service at Harvard in the summer of 1935 that my name was brought to the attention of Dr. Ray Lyman Wilbur, then president of Stanford University. Seeking a person to teach the Philosophy of Religion and to be chaplain of the university, Dr. Wilbur visited Cambridge in December. As a consequence, he asked me to meet him in Philadelphia on what was actually my thirty-fifth birthday, December 12, 1935.

While I was familiar with Wilbur's name in that he had been a member of President Herbert Hoover's cabinet as well as president of the American Medical Association, I had never before met him. At our first acquaintance he was sixty years of age and clearly at the height of his powers. An impressive man, he told me what was needed at Stanford and asked me to visit the university during the short break between semesters in the Haverford schedule. Thus occurred my first trip to the Pacific Coast, opening a new world of experience for me. Never before had I seen the Rocky Mountains or the lands beyond them. I took the Overland Limited both ways, enjoying the long train trip. At Stanford I gave the university sermon on Sunday and met later with the elder statesmen of the faculty. As I left, Dr. Wilbur told me that the appointment was mine if I wanted to have it. On the trip home I had abundant opportunity to consider carefully whether we ought to take a step of such magnitude. It meant leaving the Quaker academic pattern with which I was already familiar, and it also meant establishment in an area of the nation totally new to us. Our life in Pennsylvania was well settled and associations which we valued would inevitably be lost.

Finally, I became convinced that we ought to accept President Wilbur's invitation. Pauline met me in Philadelphia, readily concurred, and we went together to the telegraph office from which we dispatched a message of acceptance. All that we did in the next few months pointed to the largest shift which we had ever made. Settling at Stanford in June 1936, we plunged at once into a round of new duties. Our home, in close proximity to that of former President and Mrs. Hoover, gave us a splendid base of operation from the start. Soon we welcomed groups of students in the evenings, as we had done earlier at both Guilford and Haverford. The fact that we were near enough to the campus school for Martin and Arnold to walk to it was one of many reasons why Stanford seemed idyllic.

We felt at home at Stanford from the first day. We had good neighbors, the nearest being Dr. Edgar E. Robinson, chairman of the department of history. Quickly we felt close to the Hardin Craigs As professor of English and renowned Shakespeare scholar, Dr. Craig was an ornament to the university, but to me he was primarily a friend. For a long time we played golf together once a week, always without others. Though my golf never got to be very good, conversation with a wise and good man twenty-five years my senior was what I needed. We talked of his undergraduate days at Centre College, Kentucky, of Princeton, of the University of Iowa, and of many other institutions which he knew intimately, though I did not. Years later, on a freighter crossing the Pacific, I read all of Shakespeare in the handsome volume edited by Dr. Craig. After mandatory retirement at Stanford at the age of sixty-five Dr. Craig engaged in a period of even more effective teaching at the University of North Carolina at Chapel Hill. Five years later he proceeded to the University of Missouri. He is dead now, but it was from him more than from any other that I caught the basic idea of creative retirement. Retirement for Hardin Craig meant opportunity for new service. By the time of his terminal illness he had taught more than sixty years.

Ray Lyman Wilbur towered above the others at Stanford,

both physically and intellectually. Though the faculty meetings under his chairmanship were few, they were indeed memorable. Because Dr. Wilbur considered it a waste of time for scholarly men and women to argue about trivial details, the rare meetings of the faculty were devoted chiefly to memorials and to statements of policy. The memorials, in Wilbur's view, were important because they helped to maintain the spiritual continuity of university life. President Wilbur walked to the quad every morning, as I did, and sometimes we fell in step. Being the age of his own sons, I was quickly made to feel that I was almost one of them, but when I visited his office, all was business. Normally, he went on signing checks while he listened to my proposals. Always, when I finished, he gave me an answer, so that I was never in doubt. Once he stopped to explain his method. "I have many decisions to make," the Lincolnesque man said, "and some of them are wrong. But I have learned that there is something worse than a few wrong decisions, and that is *indecision.*"

One of the most important decisions we made together was that of bringing Professor Reinhold Niebuhr to the campus as West Lecturer. The brilliant lectures given by Niebuhr, published with the title *The Children of Light and the Children of Darkness*, were better attended than any previous series of lectures had been. They represent Niebuhr's thinking when he was at the top of the curve of his remarkable powers. We knew, as we attended, that we were engaged in the vision of greatness, particularly when Niebuhr said, "Man's capacity for justice makes democracy possible; but man's inclination to injustice makes democracy necessary." In one of the discussions, when an instructor asked Dr. Niebuhr who was the most original theologian of America, the visitor answered simply, "Abraham Lincoln." That surprising response, uttered in January 1944, kept working in my mind until it bore literary fruit twenty-nine years later.

e excellent photographer of Palo Alto, to whom I was
ed in England in March 1939 just after his release from
Concentration Camp. Our garden apartment on the
campus was Mr. Roth's first home in America, when
ian camera was his only possession. With his family life
photographic achievement Mr. Roth has become an
t asset to his adopted country.

San Francisco only an hour away by excellent com-
in, we came to enjoy that exciting city. On a few
in order to avoid the constant pressure of duties in the
we took a room for a day at a San Francisco hotel,
he theater at night, and came home by the late train.
month several of us who belonged to the Stanford
rneyed to the city to attend the regular dinner meet-
Chit-Chat Club. Since that particular club included
rom the University of California and other neighbor-
tions, we were thereby partially saved from academic
sm. Always there was a serious paper followed by
cussion. One member was Dr. Chauncey D. Leake,
erward visited at Galveston, where he was dean of the
of Texas Medical School. I felt fortunate to be as-
th men who knew many things which I did not know.
he last year of my service at Stanford I represented
Peace Union in the nongovernmental meeting
held in conjunction with the formation of th
tions. Because of our proximity to San Francisc
unding meetings were held, I could attend witho
ruption of my university duties. Among the wo
were present in San Francisco in the spring of 19
most impressive was General Jan Smuts of So

quarter system at Stanford made it possible fo
free quarter at some time other than summ
ny good reason for doing so. Actually, sinc

With Dr. Wilbur's generous cooperation we were able to bring to the university a number of persons of eminence. Often the visitor would preach the sermon in the university church on Sunday morning and then give public lectures on subsequent days. One of those who came in that way was my former senior colleague, Rufus M. Jones. Part of my pleasure in bringing Dr. Jones was that of observing *his* pleasure in being with Professor Augustus Murray. Jones and Murray, after graduating together at Haverford in 1885, had maintained a close friendship through more than half a century. That included Dr. Murray's residence in Washington as a spiritual mentor during the Hoover presidency. Murray was the one who introduced Herbert Hoover to classical studies when Hoover was a Stanford freshman in 1891. My little boys were greatly amused when they saw the two old men meet in our house and immediately kick each other's shins as they had done in student days.

Our neighbors, the Hoovers, regularly took a morning walk, usually coming past our house. They were always dressed impeccably and the former president always carried a walking stick. I was surprised at the innate shyness of a man who had seen so much of the world. With a few, he would talk familiarly, but invariably he fell into silence when others entered the room. Later I thought of that when I read Dr. Samuel Johnson's observation about Joseph Addison: "Before strangers, or perhaps a single stranger, he preserved his dignity by a stiff silence."

When Herbert Hoover's sister-in-law died, we went together over the mountains to the west, to the Tad Hoover home, and there we buried Tad's wife in a grave facing the ocean. When Lou Henry Hoover died, I was drawn even closer to the family. After a triumphant memorial service in the university church, we buried her in the Palo Alto Cemetery, recognizing that the vault would later be transplanted to West Branch, Iowa, as it was in 1964, subsequent to Mr. Hoover's interment.

After Mrs. Hoover died, the former president moved to New

York, living the remainder of his life in the Waldorf Towers, where I visited him from time to time, and once stayed overnight. Having promised his sons that I would conduct his memorial service, I returned from Saigon for that purpose in October 1964 and led the outdoor service at West Branch. Seventy-five thousand persons were in attendance. The good man had fortunately outlived the unfairness of those who had been fiercely judgmental, blaming him for what was really a worldwide economic storm. Never once did I hear him refer to that aspect of his career with bitterness, though it was obvious that he enjoyed the vindication which the years had brought.

My work at Stanford was sharply increased by the entrance of America into the war. New responsibilities included those for the people of Japanese descent who were in detention camps, and for the soldiers and their families who became important segments of the university. Because the influx of soldier students increased the teaching load, each professor was asked to volunteer to do something outside his own field. I volunteered to teach college algebra and did so, but it nearly killed me because there was so much catching up to do. Somehow I survived!

Theoretically I gave half of my time to teaching and half to my work as chaplain, which was advantageous in many ways. I am convinced that the academic life is more genuine if it involves a practical element, and that the spiritual life needs the intellectual to keep it honest. During most of the time, I preached at the university church three Sundays each month and taught two classes. The classes which I most enjoyed teaching were the Philosophy of Religion and Christian Classics. More and more it seemed wise to teach the latter course in our own home and thereby tighten the personal connection with the students.

The teaching of the Philosophy of Religion was essentially a new experience for me and turned out to be a highly productive one. The course enabled me to combine what I had learned in both philosophy and religion, with logic being the connecting

link. I was helped especially by devoted to physics and the other to be as tough-minded in my fie' convinced that the ways of veri God are essentially the same as sider the being of atoms. In sh truth is one! Though I was a (propose to cherish any belief m if it is not true, I kept saying

The preaching on Sunday tunity, even the location of tl Memorial Church provides th quadrangle and is meant to ƒ enterprise. Worshipers alway townspeople. The predictabl part of people like the Robir many from the sciences, was pew was always reserved for

The friendship with the ingly important in our lives. turned for medical service, wife, Mary, was effective or Two of their sons accompar one of them, Dr. Richard Pentagon.

When we heard that a Methodist Church of Pal Kennedy, we had no hint (mean. Soon, however, if spiritual and intellectual when he was elected bisl of leadership exercised Kennedy's successor, M episcopal office.

One friendship mucl

50   *Wh*

Roth, tl introduc Dachau Stanforc his Aust and his importar

With muter tr occasions universit attended

Once a faculty jo ing of the members ing institu provinciali general dis whom I aft University sociated wi

During the Churc which wer United Na where the f serious inte leaders who one of the Africa.

The four to choose m there were

delightful summer climate of Palo Alto made it almost pointless to go away for a summer vacation, we stayed whenever we could. The beautiful summers drew me to my big garden, in which I learned to adapt my thinking to the California climate. At first I was too stingy, not wanting to eliminate any shrubs, but I soon learned that with prodigious growth some destruction was required. Also, the constant necessity of watering was a conscious burden, but it became less so with the years. In fact some of my best ideas came while watering the camellias. On a few occasions we joined briefly with the Stanford colony at Fallen Leaf Lake in the Sierra Mountains and learned the health value of some contrast in elevation during the year. One of the benefits of the dry summers was that outdoor tennis could be played at least nine months of each year. My growing participation in tennis was one source of good health which has continued to this day.

During the summer and autumn of 1944 I enjoyed a semi sabbatical leave, much of which was spent in teaching. For the summer I taught at Garrett Biblical Institute, on the Northwestern University campus at Evanston, Illinois, and during the autumn I taught at Harvard. The summer brought me in touch with colleagues not known before, the most interesting of whom was Professor Nels Ferré. I had meant to employ the entire autumn as a rest period, and for that purpose had rented an old house in Newtown, Connecticut. The idea was to be close enough to New York for occasional visits, yet far enough removed to be essentially free from its strain. However, when we had barely become settled in Newtown, I received a call from Dean Sperry, asking me to teach the Philosophy of Religion at Harvard. I decided that I could do so by spending most of each week at Cambridge, with long weekends in Newtown. At Cambridge I occupied a suite in Lowell House where I was very comfortable, and taught a class of about fifty men, many of whom were mature students. One of the unexpected dividends was the invitation from Professor Alfred North Whitehead to dine with him and the Junior Society of Fellows at Eliot House. Another extra was renewed contact with Edgar Sheffield Brightman, Borden P. Bowne Professor of Philosophy at Boston University.

All during that period of relative relaxation I was thinking about my future. Should I stay permanently at Stanford University or not? I thought seriously of settling down in Newtown or some similar village, operating as a free-lance speaker, but I soon decided against it when I discovered that I missed, while there, the stimulation of an academic community. In the midst of 1945 I decided to leave Stanford, though my next step was far from clear. One reason for leaving was the retirement of President Wilbur. Also, I came to meditate more and more upon the advantages of the small college, particularly a college in which there is an unapologetic Christian commitment. I did not claim it to be the only possible pattern, but I was convinced that in our academic variety it is an option which should be kept open. I came to believe that such an institution, provided it has the right leadership, may surpass the big university, even intellectually. While I had no cause to complain of my professional opportunities at Stanford, I longed to be part of an institution of manageable dimensions in which an individual can make a real difference. My thoughts in that direction were intensified by an exceedingly generous invitation from President Frank Sparks to join the faculty of Wabash College at Crawfordsville, Indiana.

I delivered my resignation from Stanford in June 1945 with the prospect of ending my duties at Christmas, thus providing the administration with abundant time to find a successor. The subsequent six months were among the most rewarding of my entire life, partly because of the sense of liberation from urgency. There was unhurried time for me to think about the next step in my career, and I reveled in the experience.

Between the end of the summer quarter and the beginning of the autumn quarter we traveled to Indiana, chiefly because

Martin was in the naval program at Notre Dame, but also because we wanted to visit some of the Indiana colleges. When we returned to our wonderful last quarter at Stanford, we had not selected the particular college we would join, but we knew the type. We saw that excellence, far from being dependent upon bigness, may actually be incompatible with it. We were going against the stream and we did not mind doing so.

A new factor in the decision was Dr. Thomas E. Jones, who had been president of Fisk University for nearly twenty years and was now considering the presidency of Earlham, his Alma Mater. Knowing of our intended visit to Indiana in September 1945, Dr. Jones, in order to discuss the future, traveled from Nashville to Richmond, where, very quickly, we had a genuine meeting of minds. Dr. Jones said that he would accept the presidency of Earlham if I would become professor of philosophy. He explained how new life was possible in a college, depending in large measure on the ideas and team spirit of those guiding its destinies, and expressed the conviction that Earlham, with its Quaker connections and its academic history, was the ideal place to inaugurate that experiment.

Persuasive as Tom Jones was, I could not honorably neglect other invitations, which included offers at both Wabash and Swarthmore. Accordingly, we went back to California to begin my final quarter and to weigh the opportunities open to us. Early in October we decided to throw in our lot with Earlham and wrote President William C. Dennis to that effect. With the future course settled, I was all the more eager to make my last period of teaching at Stanford as good as possible. We started east in December 1945.

Because my new responsibility at Earlham did not begin until September 1946, I was free to undertake interim duties for the first eight months of that year. For the winter I divided my time between Wabash College and Garrett Institute. With the postwar influx still to come, and few undergraduates resident at

Wabash, the Wabash teaching was directed chiefly to adults in the Crawfordsville area. Nearly two hundred joined the class. There is still personal contact with some of them. The most fruitful single result of the Wabash experience was the beginning of my friendship with that remarkable man, Eli Lilly. The friendship started when I gave a speech in Indianapolis in which Mr. Lilly learned of my forthcoming visit to Germany.

It pleased me greatly, in the late spring and summer of 1946, to have an appointment to go to Europe with the Friends Ambulance Unit. The emblem which I wore, the black and red star of Quaker service, first employed in the Franco-Prussian War of 1870, was the occasion of several amusing experiences. For example, on the boat crossing from Dover to Calais a young lady, noting my emblem, asked if I were Patrick Malin. To her surprise I answered that I was not Dr. Malin but that I had on his shirt. Mrs. Malin, in Oxford, had loaned me some clothing because, lacking coupons, I had no opportunity to purchase any. Patrick Malin, also a Quaker, and later president of Robert College in Istanbul, was then engaged in refugee work.

My greatest satisfaction in going to the still war-torn areas of the Rhineland was in the distribution of the large supply of vitamin tablets which Mr. Lilly had provided. The tablets were important because in the summer of 1946 food in Germany continued to be conspicuously inadequate. The most significant feature of my European trip, however, occurred in April, on the ship from New York to Southampton. One day, while walking around the deck of the old German liner on which I was a passenger, I was stopped by a man who asked whether I was a Quaker. The man was Landrum Bolling, who asked because he saw the emblem in my lapel. When I admitted that I was a Quaker, Landrum said that he was one also, that he had been teaching political science at Beloit and was beginning two years of service in Europe with a news agency. With him on the ship were his wife, Frances, and their two small sons.

Landrum Bolling and I became friends immediately. We walked together every day for the remainder of the voyage and then met again in Oxford at the home of Dr. Henry Gillet. Naturally, I told Landrum of my decision to join the Earlham faculty, and when I explained some of the reasons for this apparently strange decision, he said he might be interested also. Accordingly, I wrote to Thomas Jones, who was still at Fisk, telling of my confidence in Landrum Bolling and suggesting him as a member of the Earlham team. Tom, because he believed me, wrote to the Bollings in Berlin, inviting them to join the Earlham faculty on their return from Europe. The consequence is that Landrum joined us two and a half years later, first as professor of political science, then as general secretary, and finally as president. He became president in 1958, following the retirement of Thomas Jones, and remained president for fifteen years before going on to his present post with the Lilly Endowment. Normally, I had not worn anything in my lapel, but I have had reason to be glad that I wore an emblem on one particular day in 1946.

While I was abroad, my family had already occupied the house which was formerly the home of Earlham presidents and which consequently was the scene of many important developments. It was there that Robert L. Kelly lived when he ended his Earlham presidency to become the first executive officer of the Association of American Colleges. Naturally, I looked forward to a wholly new development in my own teaching career, for the sense of new beginnings was in the air. Again, there were fully as many men as women in the student body, most of the male students having been matured by national service of one kind or another. Many had been in the different branches of the armed services, but others had been in Civilian Public Service. The students were ready to work and they knew why they were in college.

My chief intellectual effort at that time was directed to a new course called General Philosophy. The course was planned in my free time in Europe, partly under the influence of Whitehead's conception of what philosophical study could accomplish. Rejecting the use of a textbook *about* philosophy, I determined to introduce the students directly to works of unargued value, using my lectures on Mondays and Wednesdays to illuminate these as best I could, and arranging small discussion periods for all on Fridays. Each student was required to produce a paper each week, the topics being assigned regularly a week in advance. In the first semester there were one hundred six students in the class, every seat in the available room being occupied. The books owned by each student were Plato's *Dialogues (Apology, Crito, Phaedo, Symposium, Republic)*, Aristotle's *Metaphysics*, Descartes' *Discourse on Method*, and Whitehead's *The Function of Reason*. That was far removed from the History of Philosophy as usually taught and equally removed from the Introduction to Philosophy as I had taught it at Haverford. My new conviction was that the student, provided he could become familiar with a few really great achievements in intellectual history, could fill in the gaps on his own initiative. With many students this hypothesis has been verified in experience.

Such a complex pattern of teaching required that the lectures be as good as I could make them. Being only one element in the course, they were not sufficient, but they were necessary, as cement is necessary to a wall. Remembering the lectures of Bliss Perry in my Harvard days, I made his work my model. My new pattern included the placing of the outline of each lecture on the blackboard behind the lectern, and meticulous regard to time as a way of assuring the students of the seriousness of the undertaking. Using my father's excellent watch, it was not really difficult to be synchronized exactly with the college bells. I tried to be faithful in this respect, making the last word of each lecture coincide with the ringing of the bell. Consequently, the legend arose that the college bells were somehow connected with my brain. But I felt that everyone present had responsibilities for the next hour, and to hinder anyone in the keeping of further promises was an immoral act. Another part of the temporal pattern was the expectation of promptness on the part of the students. Each session therefore began with the opening bell. In retrospect, this emphasis on the sacredness of time seems to me essential to teaching as a high art.

With more than a hundred students in the lecture sessions, it was clearly necessary that the relation between teacher and student be really personal rather than merely public. My method was to make sure that I did not have two teaching duties in a row. Thus I could draft six or seven different students at the end of each lecture and take them with me for coffee. After the building of Teague Library as my study, that part of the academic operation was particularly fruitful, but prior to that we went together to the snack bar. Thereby it was possible in the course of a semester to establish a personal relationship with practically every member of the class.

Reading more than a hundred papers each week was not easy, but I was convinced that the steady writing was essential to the development of the mind of each student. Learning cannot proceed as a matter of passive listening. Soon I had to solicit some help on the reading of the papers, but I still took the major responsibility for the criticism of them. Though most of the students submitted papers faithfully, a few tended to fall behind and then I had to do something about it. The extreme case was that of the young man who ended the semester owing all fourteen papers. When I told him that he was failing and inquired the reason, he replied, "I'll tell you. My standard of excellence is so high that I cannot bear to hand in the poor things of which I am capable." In listening to him I understood better than ever before the deep danger of perfectionism; the ideal best can in fact become the enemy of the concrete good.

One new feature of my Earlham teaching was the introduction of outside examiners. For me to judge my own product seemed not sufficiently objective. The first outsider brought in was Professor Paul Weiss, then of Yale, who impressed the students both by his scholarly competence and his interest in them as persons. Like an athletic coach, I tried to prepare my students for the fray, for they and I were on the same side. We also employed outside examiners for the final comprehensive examination, without which no degree in philosophy was granted.

In the past at Earlham all of the philosophy teaching had been done by one man, but President Jones soon realized that I needed help. A succession of colleagues followed, to whom I became indebted. The one with the longest tenure was Grimsley T. Hobbs, later president of Guilford College, who was my associate for fourteen years.

The dream which we were developing at Earlham began to attract attention across the country. One consequence was a request from Paul Davis, educational adviser to the *Reader's Digest,* for an article, "Why I Chose a Small College." It appeared in the *Digest* for September 1956, reprints being widely distributed by other colleges. I was also invited to give an address on "The Idea of a College" at the annual meeting of the Association of American Colleges, held in Cincinnati in 1949 under the guidance of Dr. Guy Snavely, Dr. Kelly's successor as executive secretary. This developed finally into a book by the same title published in 1959. A brief statement of this philosophy, with the title "The Reason for Earlham," has appeared each year for two decades in the *Earlham Catalogue.* We put the philosophy first because, even before the phrase was popularized, we believed that ideas have consequences.

As we worked together, Professor Hobbs did the chief teaching in the History of Philosophy and also Ethics, while I taught both Logic and the Philosophy of Religion. It pleased me to have logic students who were concentrating in either mathematics or one of the natural sciences. At Earlham a sense of tension has never developed between the scientific and the religious view of reality, partly because the same kind of tough-minded thinking is expected in both fields. In our first big drive for capital funds we presented the need of both a meetinghouse and a science hall, referring to the combination as a fertile cross.

From the beginning President Jones graciously gave me responsibilities beyond those of actual teaching. The two chief tasks were the planning of convocations and the recruitment of new teaching faculty. We sought to lift the convocations to a uniformly high level, realizing that required attendance laid upon us the responsibility of making each occasion the very best possible. One of the first speakers under the new plan was Professor Hardin Craig, who gave his famous address, "Renaissance Now." I watched for new men and women wherever I went, convinced that the best college is the one with the best teachers. In nearly every case President Jones cooperated by offering contracts to those in whom I had reason to believe.

My teaching career was interrupted in 1954 and 1955 by a temporary appointment in Washington. President Eisenhower, concerned that the United States Information Agency should emphasize some of the spiritual roots of our way of life, supported an enlargement of its staff, intended to achieve that purpose, and I was asked to guide the new effort. In line with his unfailing generosity President Jones suggested a leave of absence which I gladly took. In actual practice my teaching continued on another level in that I was asked to lecture with some regularity to the officers assigned to foreign service. One by-product was the friendship of President Eisenhower, who, after I had preached the sermon at the National Presbyterian Church with the Eisenhowers present, invited me to the White House and later, after his retirement, to Gettysburg.

During the Washington interlude I visited the Earlham campus at least once each month. During part of my absence the classes for which I had been responsible were taught by my former student, William Orr, who is now on the faculty of Centenary College, Hackettstown, New Jersey.

After my return to Earlham in 1956 it was understood that I was free to travel widely, to speak in other colleges and universities, and to write. President Jones and I trusted each other, and for several years, until his recent death, we lived side by side on the edge of the campus. With the pattern of freedom already established, President Bolling suggested, upon the occasion of my retirement in June 1966, that instead of being Professor Emeritus I be named Professor-at-Large. I like the title immensely, for it means that in spite of freedom the connection which I have prized is intact.

4. Author

A word is the operative symbol of a relation between two minds.

Sir Walter Raleigh

The summer of 1935, when I was thirty-four years old, was a crucial one in my career. Earlier, I had considered trying to write a publishable book, but had not been satisfied that I was ready to do so. Then in 1935, as acting chaplain of Harvard University, I had my chance. Following my early morning responsibilities in Appleton Chapel, I was relatively free for the remainder of the day and had the use of Dean Sperry's spacious study in which to do my own work. With the Widener Library at hand I was presented with an ideal opportunity, and I resolved to take advantage of it.

Prior to 1935 I had published a few magazine articles and had filled numerous notebooks with material designed for my own eyes. I was already associate editor of *The Friend* and was scheduled to assume the editorship in October of that year, in addition to my Haverford professorship. The writing of editorials and special articles had increased my facility in composition. As I look now at my youthful diaries and journals, I see that I had long been devoted to the production of the written word. Thus on February 18, 1922, when twenty-one years old, I had written in my journal, "I have been thinking about my future today, and feel now that I want to make writing a profession."

The book composed in Memorial Church, Harvard, in the summer of 1935 was entitled *The Essence of Spiritual Religion* and was dedicated to Rufus Jones. Having no idea then that the volume would have thirty successors, I let it go out of print in a year or so, but it will now be reissued. The major topics are those of worship, ministry, authority, revelation, and the sacramental view of life. Perhaps the most surprising chapter to the contemporary reader is the one devoted to the ministry, entitled "The Abolition of the Laity." The key sentence, which I have since elaborated many times in many situations, was as follows: "If we could see our daily tasks as part of the ministry, if we could know that what we do is valuable only as it helps in some way to arouse the sense of God's Presence, then all life would be infinitely raised."

When Dean Sperry, while still abroad, read the manuscript of my first book, he graciously agreed to write a foreword. Meantime, I had sent the book to Harper & Brothers. The reader can understand something of my ignorance about publishing when I say that at that time I did not even know the name of the religion editor at Harper. I soon learned, however, that this capable man was Eugene Exman, because, while I was still in Cambridge, he wrote, saying that the book was accepted. I was of course overjoyed, and ever since I have been happy about the publishing contact thus established. How different my life would have been had I addressed the envelope to some other publisher, as I seriously considered doing. Gene Exman quickly became my friend as well as my editor, and the friendship has continued warmly to this day. We have enjoyed visiting the Exmans in their beautiful home on Cape Cod.

The average reader is often surprised to learn of the genuine friendliness which can develop between an author and a publisher. Never, in our case, has the connection been merely or even primarily a business one. When my wife and I visit New York, we usually go first to the Harper offices because we want to see our friends, one of the most valued of whom is Eleanor Jordan, long Gene Exman's associate editor. With the exception of my Swarthmore Lecture, published in London by Allen and Unwin, all of my books have been produced, so far as their original form is concerned, by the firm now known as Harper & Row. The fellowship extends through the publisher to fellow authors. The most delightful example of this experience is my friendship with the late Harry Emerson Fosdick. Dr. Fosdick and I were drawn together because we shared the same editor and because of my collaboration in selecting the title of Dr. Fosdick's autobiography, *The Living of These Days.*

After the first sweet taste of book publication it soon became obvious that the habit tends to be a permanent one. As I proceeded to write either the editorials in *The Friend* or subsequent books, I was determined to write as well as I could on each occasion, following the rule of John Milton, who expressed the desire that he might "leave something so written to aftertimes, as they should not willingly let it die."

As my confidence in the House of Harper grew, the time came when prospective books were fully discussed and agreed upon before the beginning of actual writing. Sometimes a Harper editor has initiated a topic and I have tried to respond. Normally Harper has encouraged me to choose my own titles, though editors have sometimes chosen between alternative titles which I have suggested. I came very quickly to appreciate the importance of titles, realizing that some good books are hindered in circulation by poor ones. I suppose that my most satisfactory title is *The Company of the Committed*, but the reader should know that such a title comes only after long continued intellectual struggle. Indeed, ninety-nine titles were discarded before that particular one occurred to me.

Some readers may wonder how an author writes. In my case all is done longhand with a fountain pen, with ink that flows effortlessly. By this method I avoid the mechanics of the typewriter, and the speed of the pen seems to match the speed of my mind. Writing all morning in this fashion, I can without strain produce two thousand five hundred words. Because unbroken speed helps to create smoothness of style, I make only a minimum of corrections as I produce the first draft. Later, of course, especially after the chapters are typed, I substitute, delete, and add to my heart's content. But it is the original writing which is both exhilarating and energy-consuming! I can support Dr. Johnson's famous words, "The production of something where nothing was before, is an act of greater energy than the expansion or decoration of the thing produced." The perennial advice, therefore, is "Invent first and embellish later." I find that my scissors are among the most used of the literary tools on my desk because, after a chapter is in typescript, it becomes obvious to me that certain lines will fit better in some place other than that in which they were originally located. Accordingly, on the second typing, one page may be made up of a number of small parts clipped together.

I should like to convey to my readers something of the joy of writing which I regularly experience. The very act of writing can be remarkably creative. When I sit down with the paper in front of me, I know in general what I want to say, but I seldom know the details. As the ideas are expressed in written form, however, they begin to grow and to develop by their own inherent logic. Always I am a bit surprised by what has been written, for I have become in some sense an instrument.

Many have asked why I do not dictate. The crucial reason is that I need to see what I am producing, and what is on a tape cannot be seen. In many instances it is better to alter the phrase immediately, as soon as I have put it on paper. It may be entirely satisfactory to dictate a simple letter either to a stenographer or to a machine, but the production of a book is something wholly different. I have heard of books being dictated, but in every case I think they would have been better books if they had been written. The art of revision is important in the production of a worthy style. The biggest single step in revision is elimination; I soon learned that it is what is left out that counts. As there are very few speeches which are not improved by deletion of material that does not contribute to the total effort, so it is with books. A good book must be the residue, often with as much eliminated as retained. A book which appears to be padded, especially with unnecessary quotations, is intrinsically a poor one.

Each author must learn at what time of day he operates most efficiently. Being a morning person, I make it a rule not to write after noon. Sometimes I find I can revise in the afternoon or evening because that can be done when my energy is not at its peak, but on the whole not even this is part of my practice. There are plenty of other things to do in the afternoons and evenings, including the reading of books, engaging in exercise, and conversation with friends. But the author who takes his profession seriously will expect to be invaded by ideas at all times and in all places whatever he may be doing. The important thing, then, is never to be without pen and paper, for the ideas are as fugitive as they are precious.

Most of my books, produced in the last twenty years, have been written either in my study at Earlham College or at Pen Point, my writing cabin in the Pocono Mountains of Pennsylvania, near Buck Hill Falls. The writing cabin, which was completed in 1951, has given me a place of unusual seclusion. Situated on the edge of the wilderness, the cabin has no telephone, the chief articles of furniture being a big pine desk and a Harvard chair. At Earlham my study, Teague Library, is a small separate building constructed in 1958 by the generosity of the late Edward Gallahue of Indianapolis. Now that I have given my mountain retreat to my children, all of my current writing is done in the campus study. But it was not always so! I have had to employ the time that has been available, whatever the location has been. The first chapter of the *Earlham Catalogue*, called "The Reason for Earlham," was composed in the Midway Airport, Chicago, after a flight had been canceled. The obvious golden text is, "Be ye therefore ready."

How long does it take to write a book? No author knows how to answer that question because its meaning is seldom clear. If reference is made to the genesis of ideas, almost any worthwhile book necessitates several years. However, if the actual work of putting pen to paper is meant, it is a matter of only a few weeks. In every case, when I get the idea for a potential publication, I employ one or more manila folders in the collection of thoughts, quotations, epigraphs, etc. Day after day I transfer notes from my breast-pocket notebook to the appropriate folder. Later, when the division into chapters has become fairly clear, the notes are divided accordingly, each potential chapter having its own folder.

My first serious writing at Stanford University was an enlargement of my Swarthmore Lecture in a book entitled *The Knowledge of God*, published at the end of 1939. But I saw that book as only a beginning in a new field. For years I had been collecting notes on the philosophy of religion until I had a stack many inches high. The day came when I sat on the floor of my Stanford study and divided all of the notes into eighteen piles. Each pile was inserted into a separate folder and each eventually became a chapter. There was naturally one folder on Immortality, one on the Problem of Evil, one on Science, etc. The separation of the notes was the hardest work that I had ever done. Then there was the problem of how to find the time to engage in this rigorous kind of writing. Unable to write in my office because of constant interruptions, I used a little room near the top of the stairs in the University Library and wrote there two half-days a week for about a year. Because of the possibility of some genuine emergency arising, only my wife knew where I was working. I found to my satisfaction that there were no demands that could not wait for a few hours.

A public man, though he is necessarily available at many times, must learn to hide. If he is always available, he is not worth enough when he *is* available. I once wrote a chapter in the Cincinnati Union Station, but that was itself a form of hiding because nobody knew who the man with the writing pad was. Consequently nobody approached me during five wonderful hours until the departure of the next train for Richmond. We must use the time which we have because even at best there is never enough.

The Logic of Belief, which was given the subtitle "An Introduction to the Philosophy of Religion," represented my best effort in a field in which I sought to be academically competent. The careful study of the works of Archbishop William Temple had already influenced me greatly and had set the tone of my reasoning. I believed then, and I believe now, that Dr. Temple's Gifford Lectures, *Nature, Man and God,* constitute one of the intellectual achievements of our century. When *The Philosophy of Religion* was published in 1957, some paragraphs of *The Logic of Belief* were incorporated in it and Harper decided to allow the earlier volume to go out of print. It was in the earlier volume that I first adopted the practice of selecting an epigraph to head each chapter, a practice which I have followed in the thirty succeeding years.

At Stanford, in addition to books, I was writing a few articles, seeking consciously to reach readers through the secular magazines rather than the religious ones because I believed that the ideas would have a wider impact thereby. The most important was an essay published by *The Atlantic Monthly* in the December 1940 issue. The essay, called "The Quaker Way," dealt with the issues involved in the war.

About that time I wrote an article for the *Christian Science Monitor*, and my young son, Arnold, was immensely pleased that I could express my thinking in newspaper style. Why not, he asked, alter my style so as to reach the average literate person? Those were not his exact words, but that is what he meant. At the same time I was beginning to read the works of C. S. Lewis, whose complete liberation from the bondage of academic jargon I much admired. Lewis dealt with the most profound questions in a style of utmost clarity. I determined to try to do in America something of what C. S. Lewis was doing in England and soon saw the necessity of the small book. What size of book will the ordinary, busy, yet thoughtful person pick up and read? I concluded that such a book would have to be large enough to win respect and small enough to be read, if necessary, in one sitting. It would therefore be a book of slightly more than a hundred pages, ideally limited to five chapters. The result was the production of my first book of a particular type, *The Predicament of Modern Man.* The book attracted wide attention, partly because it had the generous public support of men of the character of Reinhold Niebuhr and Harry Emerson Fosdick. Its appearance in shortened form in the *Reader's Digest* brought correspondence so heavy that it took me some time before I finally was able to respond to every letter.

It was the first of my books to reach the general public, and was really an essay in the breakdown and restoration of civilization. In writing it, I had consciously disciplined myself to be clear, and to follow a logical sequence, so that Chapter 1 led to Chapter 2, Chapter 2 to Chapter 3, and so on through the book. The single idea that was most exciting to me was that of the impossibility of a cut-flower civilization. I still remember how the figure hit me in February 1944 and where I was walking when I thought of the title to which the idea led. The key passage, which appeared in Chapter 3 on "The Impotence of Ethics," was as follows:

The terrible danger of our time consists in the fact that ours is a *cut-flower civilization*. Beautiful as cut flowers may be, and much as we may use our ingenuity to keep them looking fresh for a while, they will eventually die, and they die because they are severed from their sustaining roots. We are trying to maintain the dignity of the individual apart from the deep faith that every man is made in God's image and is therefore precious in God's eyes.

The book was published in August 1944, its publication being the single most crucial external event in my life. There were many consequences, including those which appeared in succeeding volumes from my pen. Nearly all of the ideas, which I have subsequently elaborated, exist in germ in that book.

In 1945 I determined again to produce something of a different character, convinced that an author is more effective if he does not allow himself to be limited to one particular type of book. Accordingly, I worked on the prayers of Dr. Samuel Johnson with the intention of making those genuine classics of devotion available to students and other interested people. The need arose out of the class in Christian Classics, in which the few Johnson prayers available to contemporary readers only whetted the appetite for more. I had noticed, while still a college student, that Dr. Fosdick, in his book *The Meaning of Prayer*, had quoted Samuel Johnson. Indeed, the very first prayer presented in Fosdick's fine book is Johnson's prayer on Neglect of Duty. In reading Boswell's *Life* I had of course seen a few more of the famous prayers and had been struck especially with the prayer which Johnson composed when, in 1750, he began to write the *Rambler*. Since the collection edited by Dr. George Strahan in 1785 with the title *Prayers and Devotions* had long been out of print, I knew it could not be purchased and therefore I decided to edit a new volume. I presented one hundred prayers in groups referring to work, to his wife's death, to New Years, etc., and also wrote a long introduction. The volume, *Doctor Johnson's*

Prayers, after a preliminary local production in 1945, was published in 1947 both by Harper in America and by the Student Christian Movement Press in England. Before final publication I had the privilege of reading the prayers in Johnson's handwriting in the library of Pembroke College, Oxford, where most of the manuscripts are preserved.

Another change in style came in my last six months of living and working in California, in the production of a small book reinterpreting the Ten Commandments. The decision to write the book came suddenly as I sat in one of the San Francisco meetings concerned with the formation of the United Nations. It occurred to me that world reconstruction, about which we were conferring, is impossible apart from a moral basis, and that in this regard the Decalogue is as pertinent as ever. With speed came the conviction that all of the commandments could be reinterpreted in positive form. I saw, for example, that the only reason why theft is evil is that ownership is good, and that adultery is wrong precisely because fidelity is right. As in most of my books, the essence of that volume was spoken before it was written. The immense advantage of reversing the conventional practice and speaking prior to writing is that this method is, in reality, the experimental method. By trying out the ideas vocally, the speaker can watch for reactions and can profit accordingly. Though the spoken and the written style are very different, the former helps to achieve clarity in the latter. Before committing the book to writing, I gave it as ten consecutive sermons in the university church, the published volume, when it appeared early in 1946, being entitled *Foundations for Reconstruction.* A revised edition appeared in 1961, and a paperback edition, produced by Word, Inc., was issued in 1972.

The bound volumes of *The Friend,* 1935–1945, are among the most prized possessions of my library. One hesitation about leaving the Philadelphia area in 1936 to go to Palo Alto arose from my editorship of the oldest Quaker magazine in the world.

Because it seemed a shame to give up the editorship, I tried to avoid doing so. Fortunately, the board of the magazine agreed that I continue as the writer of the editorial articles because the associate editor, Richard Wood, lived near Philadelphia and could attend to day-by-day management. The change in physical location turned out to be unimportant because my editorials usually were sent by mail anyway, and by the use of airmail they could be posted on the same day as when I taught at Haverford.

Feeling keenly the dignity of *The Friend*, I sought to maintain a literary standard in every issue. Now, as I peruse the bound volumes, I realize that the essays printed for the ten-year period of my editorship beginning in October 1935 really provided me with a valuable proving ground. Many of the periodical productions were later developed more fully and appeared, in altered form, in books. My gratitude to Richard Wood for his unfailing helpfulness during our years of editorial partnership is something I take this opportunity to express publicly.

I ended my duties with *The Friend* in 1945, convinced that the increase of responsibilities incident to joining the staff at Earlham College would make further editorial writing impractical. While it lasted, the discipline of regular bi-weekly writing was as helpful as it was demanding.

The first book which I undertook after my removal to Indiana, entitled *Alternative to Futility*, was written at Earlham in the early summer of 1947, after one full year of teaching. It was produced with a greater sense of exhilaration than I have known in any other literary effort. At the time of publication, February 1948, the material was given as the Scarbrough Lectures at Austin, Texas. The main theme of the book was the amplification of the final chapter of *The Predicament of Modern Man*, "The Necessity of a Redemptive Society." Because the central idea was one for which many people were ready, numerous groups with a variety of names were formed. Several of them adopted the phrase coined in the book, "The Fellowship of the

Concerned." In that book I first tried to describe in some detail the kind of Christian fellowship which is both possible and necessary if the Christian Cause is to endure and to be effective. The book has been referred to as one of the earliest emphases on the theme of Church Renewal.

After the completion of the lectures at Austin we went as a family to the Heart-of-the-Hills Inn, west of Kerrville, Texas, in order for me to write without distractions. There I wrote, under exceedingly happy circumstances, the volume later called *The Common Ventures of Life*. My purpose was to deal with experiences which are humanly universal or nearly so: Marriage, Birth, Work, and Death. To join a mate, to produce a child, to find a worthwhile work to do, and finally to die—it is to these experiences that we are called. All can be spoiled and all can be glorified. The religion mankind needs is the kind which can dignify and magnify these elements of common life.

Each evening in front of a blazing fire and at the invitation of the innkeeper, I read aloud what I had written that day. The listeners were both our fellow guests and the maids. Never before had I enjoyed that particular opportunity, and it is one which has never been repeated. The inevitability of the title did not penetrate my thinking until the following June, when I realized that each of the four experiences is in a profound sense a genuine leap.

The Life We Prize was written under other skies but in equally appealing circumstances. Because my duties at the college required only one semester a year, we decided to spend most of the autumn of 1950 in the British Isles. To make possible a concentrated period of writing, we settled at Charney Manor, a Quaker guest house located in a quaint Berkshire village fourteen miles west of Oxford. Charney is said to be the oldest inhabited house of England, the exposed oak beams under which I wrote having endured for more than seven hundred years. There I could write without disturbance and there I completed the first draft of my only book devoted to moral philosophy. Recently I have been able to write a new opening chapter in order to update the historical references, and the book has been brought out in paperback by Word, Inc., who have purchased the publishing rights from Harper & Row. The bulk of the book is devoted to ethical thinking, but would not be complete without the final chapter called "A Basic Faith." The book, which was rewritten in detail after our return to America, was published in 1951, the preface being dated in June of that year. I have sometimes pointed to that book when asked to name the one by which I am most willing to be judged.

After the major effort represented by *The Life We Prize* I returned for a while to the small book pattern, bringing out three volumes between 1952 and 1955. The first, *Your Other Vocation*, was written to help fill the vacuum created by the lack of books on the lay ministry. The second, *The Recovery of Family Life*, developed more fully one chapter in the former volume and was published with my wife, Pauline, as co-author shortly before her final illness and death. The third, *Declaration of Freedom*, endeavored to delineate the American conception of disciplined freedom and was given as the Colver Lectures at Brown University. Much of the material was used on the Voice of America.

The Philosophy of Religion, which sought to carry on and to update what I had done in *The Logic of Belief*, was written in the early part of 1956 after my work with the United States Information Agency had been completed and before I returned to active teaching in September. It was my most ambitious effort up to that time. Following it I turned to three literary tasks wholly different from either the textbook type or the small book type: a volume of sermons, a book on educational philosophy, and an experiment in devotional literature. I had never issued a volume of sermons, but my wife, Virginia, soon after our marriage, expressed the hope that I should do so. Most of the actual writing was performed on shipboard between Montreal and London in the late spring of 1958. Each day I wrote on deck, while Virginia typed the manuscript in our stateroom. It was possible to produce the text at top speed because all of the addresses had been given vocally already. Traveling in England, we revised the manuscript at many different locations, particularly Epworth, and finally at St. Augustine's College, Canterbury. It pleased me to dedicate the volume, entitled *The Yoke of Christ*, "to Virginia, who would not let the idea rest."

The next book, devoted to educational philosophy, was produced as the clarification of an academic dream, the same dream which had brought me to Earlham. Completed in 1959, it represented more than a decade of experience in the effort to give embodiment to an appealing vision. The title, *The Idea of a College*, was intended to remind readers of *The Idea of a University* by Cardinal Newman, whose portrait hung on my wall.

My one experiment in devotional writing, *Confronting Christ*, was based upon the conviction that direct acquaintance with Jesus Christ, in so far as this is possible, is the best known way of deepening any individual life. I had already been struck by the potent words of Thomas à Kempis, "Meditate on His life, and thou wilt be ashamed to find how far removed thou art from His perfection." Finding myself thankful for the very existence of the four Gospels, and particularly of Mark, I conceived the plan of dividing the oldest Gospel into what are its sixty constituent parts, instead of the conventional sixteen chapters, adding a brief commentary to each, and challenging the reader to face Christ in this manner for sixty consecutive days. In preparation I sat with my former teacher of Greek, Professor William E. Berry, as we made our own translation of all of Mark. Actually, the printed form of the Gospel in the book is that of the Revised Standard Version, but the task of dealing with it in the original, as we did, was eminently worthwhile.

About a year later I returned to the small book pattern with

The Company of the Committed, the volume which has now been more widely distributed than any other that I have written. It picked up the theme of *Alternative to Futility* after thirteen years, stressing the important idea that it is not possible to be a Christian alone. Before it was published, the ideas of the book were given as lectures in various places in both the United States and Europe. I was especially glad to speak on the theme of the redemptive fellowship to men and women of our armed services in France, Germany, and Italy. When the book appeared in October 1961, Cass Canfield, the president of the House of Harper, gave a luncheon for me at the Century Club in New York, thereby celebrating twenty-five years of teamwork between publisher and author. When Mr. Canfield asked me to suggest names for those to be invited, I included both former colleagues and my three sons, two of whom spoke spontaneously at the table. I felt again that it was good to be associated with a firm for which I had unqualified respect.

While we were in Germany, the plan of another and wholly different type of book was originated. Having long given the course called General Philosophy, I knew that I ought sometime to write a book with that title. It was surprising to learn that after all of the thousands of volumes on philosophy, not one, so far as we could discover, had ever used that obvious title. What I wanted to produce was a thorough and scholarly book which could become an instrument for study on the part of people working alone, as well as those involved in classes. I knew that the book would have to discuss all of the major themes of human thinking, including the mystery of knowledge, the meaning of persons, the relation of mind and body, and the being of God. It was not my purpose to cover again the arguments presented in *The Philosophy of Religion*, but to deal instead with the broader field of inquiry, which underlies all scientific, aesthetic, and moral reflection. I knew from the start that the book would have to begin, as my own philosophic quest had begun, with

"The Heritage of Socrates." My purpose at every point was to guide students to the sources, including the *Dialogues* of Plato. As in my course of the same name, I hoped to lead thoughtful seekers beyond "knowledge about" to "acquaintance with."

The clear vision of what would be a highly demanding venture came to me as I walked on the famous *Philosophenweg* above Heidelberg. Looking across the Neckar River, I was inspired by the skyline of the ancient city, with its castle, and I was conscious of the many who had walked where I was walking. I determined then and there to start the most arduous task of my academic career, reminding myself that at sixty I ought to be ready. It helped me to realize that I was at the very age which Plato had attained when he wrote the dialogue which is my favorite of all, the *Theaetetus*. The date was April 16, 1961, and the place was a seat on the Philosopher's Way. As my wife and others of our party walked on, I sat and wrote the opening paragraph of the book which thereafter occupied my time for many subsequent months until it was published in 1963. The writing required, of course, unusual attention to detail, including the preparation of specialized appendices intended to save student time. These contained biographical notes on philosophers, notes on philosophical systems, and a classified bibliography.

As I wrote *General Philosophy* I was constantly aware of the paradox of my position. Like Plato in his celebrated Seventh Letter, I was convinced that the most important truths cannot be put into a book. Yet I knew that Plato wrote the *Dialogues*, and there is no serious doubt that some of the ideas expressed in them, particularly the later ones, are his own. Since we cannot escape the paradox, we must learn to live with it, determined never to lose the beneficent tension. It was therefore not surprising that for the opening epigraph I turned to that master of paradox, Blaise Pascal, repeating his words, "Man is obviously made to think. It is his whole dignity and his whole merit; and his whole duty is to think as he ought."

When *General Philosophy* had been published, I sought again a change of literary pace. Thus my next two books, published in 1964 and 1965, were directed to different aspects of the life and character of Jesus Christ. I recognized how little most people, including those who call themselves Christians, know about Him. The first book was devoted to Christ's use of humor, and the second to His theory and practice of prayer. The former was entitled *The Humor of Christ*, and the latter, *The Lord's Prayers*. Both fell within the 128-page limit which Harper & Row had encouraged.

The book on Christ's use of humor was the outgrowth of an experience in our home on the Guilford College campus when our eldest son, then aged four, began to laugh while the Scripture was being read. It was something of a revelation to see that a little child would appreciate humor of which sober adults were totally unaware. In subsequent years I kept watching for signs of laughter in the Gospels and soon realized that such signs are far from rare. What gratified me most was that certain passages, among which the story of the Unjust Steward is eminent, are understandable upon the hypothesis that Christ was joking, while they are mystifying, and even damaging, without this interpretation. I was greatly pleased when Harry Emerson Fosdick wrote in his review of the book, "I venture to think that in the interpretation of certain especially difficult passages this book will turn out to be epoch-making." The book has been the occasion for many letters from total strangers, who have reported that they have been helped by seeing Christ in a new light and thereby have been freed from a false stereotype.

The Lord's Prayers was my attempt to reflect deeply upon the tremendous fact that Jesus prayed. Like others, I feel now, as I have always felt, genuine difficulties in accepting the efficacy of prayer, but the difficulties begin to vanish in the light of Christ's own reported experience. I prepared for the writing of the book by marking every passage I could find in the Gospels with any reference to prayer. The basic idea came to me in St. Paul's Church, Richmond, Virginia, in March 1964, and the manuscript was produced in the writing cabin in the Pocono Mountains, being sent to the publishers in August.

For many years, both at Haverford and at Earlham, I had taught a course in Quakerism, and finally it seemed right to put the essentials of the course into written form. The result was not a detailed history of Quakerism, but rather the portraiture of a movement. The recounting of the history had already been done so thoroughly by Rufus Jones and others that it was not needed, but the portraiture was badly needed, partly because of the grotesque misconceptions which are widely current. The title *The People Called Quakers* was chosen because that was the precise appellation employed in the seventeenth century by William Penn, Robert Barclay, and many other Quaker leaders. Knowing the terrible danger of a sect within a sect, I made a conscious effort to be fair to all aspects of the Quaker Movement. The fact that I had had opportunity to become acquainted with all of the major current brands of Quakerism, on both sides of the Atlantic, made this particular emphasis possible. Fortunately, the book has now been reproduced in an inexpensive paperback by Friends United Press.

After the big book on Quakerism it was time for another small book, especially one which could elaborate further the wonders, dangers, and potentialities of the Christian fellowship. The result was *The Incendiary Fellowship*, written at Pen Point in the summer of 1966 and published in 1967. The book took its title from the relatively unfamiliar words of Christ, "I came to cast fire upon the earth" (Luke 12:49), and included a new hymn, "Baptism by Fire," which I wrote in 1966. To my satisfaction, the hymn is now used by various branches of the Christian faith, usually sung to the Welsh tune *Hyfrydol*, and it also appears in the new hymn books both of the Presbyterian Churches and the Evangelical Covenant Church of America. My hope for the

book was that it would bring together various facets of the
Church Renewal movement, since the discussion of Church
Renewal had by that time progressed sufficiently to make some-
thing of a consensus possible.

When the autumn quarter of 1966 came, I wanted to be far
removed from the Earlham campus, partly in order to give every
freedom to Professor Robert Horn, my successor in the philosophy department. While the students were gathering in September, I was spending peaceful days at Pen Point, and then, soon
afterward, my wife and I flew to England, where for several
months I was free to complete what was essentially a lifework,
the biography of Robert Barclay. We lived most of the time in
London at the Cora Hotel on Upper Woburn Place, in close
proximity to valuable libraries, particularly Friends House Library where the actual writing was done. The librarian, Edward
Milligan, generously gave me the use of an alcove where I could
surround myself with the materials which I needed, without the
necessity of their constant return to the shelves.

My decision to try to do justice to Barclay had come first in
1939 when, as a Fellow of Woodbrooke, I discovered Robert
Barclay's Notebook. To my surprise and dismay certain parts
that appeared to be relevant were in code. Since the code had
no similarity to any contemporary shorthand, neither I nor any
of my friends could decipher it or even distinguish between top
and bottom. I felt keenly the need of producing a thorough
treatment of the life and thought of a man of Barclay's eminence. After all, he was the most respected of all Quaker intellectuals for three hundred years; he was nonresident Governor
of New Jersey; he collaborated with King James II in bringing
about freedom from religious persecution. But I could not safely
proceed without knowing what the shorthand notebook said. It
might be trivial, but how could I be sure? Finally, after long
continued failure, Douglas G. Lister, then living in Ethiopia,
appeared one day at Friends House Library and offered his

services. Being one of the most skilled persons of the world in seventeenth-century shorthand, he was able to decode the Barclay system. By the time of my retirement and temporary residence in England, Mr. Lister had also moved to England, so that we could collaborate with relative ease. Soon we translated every line, and I could proceed with confidence in writing the book which I had planned for nearly twenty-eight years. The coded material actually helped in the understanding of Barclay's intellectual development.

The story of the production of *Robert Barclay* is something of a thriller from beginning to end. In April 1967, after the main chapters of the book had been composed and typed, I made one last effort to see if the frequently mentioned Diary of Barclay could be found. By a fortunate series of steps too numerous to mention here, two Diary volumes were found in the home of Mrs. Robert Barclay at Bury Hill, near Dorking. I had visited Bury Hill fruitlessly in 1939, but the 1967 visit was more rewarding than I had expected it to be. The chief valuables, including, besides the Diaries, original letters from William Penn and Princess Elizabeth of the Rhine, are now deposited in the Strong Room of Friends House Library. The Barclay labor was a long one, but it was finally worthwhile.

The years between 1968 and 1972 were devoted largely to the production of four more small books designed to give guidance or support to the Christian Cause. The first, called *A Place to Stand*, dealt directly with the problem of belief. I had come to feel acutely the lack of positive belief on the part of millions, including many church members. I concluded that it is possible to present, in small compass as C. S. Lewis had done earlier, a faith which meets the demands of rational examination. The Christian, I was convinced, must be able to meet all opposition, and he cannot do so unless he has a firm base from which to operate. Like Archimedes, he cannot lift anything unless his center is solid.

The essence of my strategy in writing the book lay in the selection of a starting point. I found that if we begin by talking of God, people turn us off because they do not understand who He is, but that if we begin with Christ, there are many who are ready and willing to listen. The strategy is to start with the known, this being the position of greatest dependability. Then later, as a consequence, we can move on to belief in God, which is credible because Christ believed. Once we start with the conviction that Christ is trustworthy, many of the problems fade, but without such a starting point we can do very little. In short, I took seriously the notion that Christ leads us to God; *if God is not, then Christ was wrong.* My judgment is that *A Place to Stand* may be read longer than any other of my thirty books.

The second book in the series, called *The New Man for Our Time,* was an effort to help to solve the prevalent problem of polarization in the Christian Movement, particularly that between the activists and the pietists. The volume has had a very wide reading and has, I believe, contributed somewhat to the solution of the problem. I decided to dedicate it to my loyal associate, Robert Pitman, who has for sixteen years greatly increased my productivity. In book after book he has, along with my wife, turned manuscript into typescript with unfailing patience. He has been my literary colleague, increasingly willing to offer suggestions about changes in both style and content.

The third book, called *The Future of the Christian* and published in 1971, was written to encourage Christians in the face of the widespread prediction of inevitable decline. Disgusted with the superficiality of those who say blandly that we are in the post-Christian age, I began to contemplate seriously the amazing fact of Christian survival. The more I thought, the less I believed that modern man can destroy what Nero and others like him could not eradicate. Not only does the record of history give evidence that Christianity will endure; it also indicates the

continuance of the Church. The forms of the Church will undoubtedly be altered in various ways, but Christ's prediction that
the powers of death cannot prevail against it makes as much
sense now as ever.

One of the best evidences of the continued vitality of the
Church of Christ lies in its world-wide character. This came to
me with vividness during a slow journey around the world from
November 1970 to February 1971. Having long listened to the
conventional arguments against the World Mission, I became
convinced that they could be answered, and the fourth book in
the series, called *The Validity of the Christian Mission*, was my
effort to provide an answer. The concept of mission is intrinsic
because no true Christian can be content to hold his faith to
himself; whatever he really prizes he is bound to share. As I
visited the brave fellowships of Asia and Africa, I understood
better the words of Emil Brunner, "The Church exists by mission, as fire exists by burning."

The study of the religious thinking of Abraham Lincoln was
of a character radically different from anything which I had ever
attempted before. Hints dropped by both Dean Willard Sperry
and Professor Reinhold Niebuhr kept working in my mind.
What if Lincoln has something to say to us which the professional theologians do not know? We are not rich enough intellectually or spiritually to neglect any of the help which we can
get, especially when it comes from those who are generally
acknowledged to be the wisest and the best. Accordingly, I set
to work and stayed with the subject over a period of eight years
before I was ready to do the actual writing in the summer of
1972.

The books referring to Lincoln are so numerous that no individual can read them all, but he does not need to do so. What
is much more important is to read what Lincoln himself wrote
and said. It took me a long time to see the sequence in ideas,
to understand the growth, and to be ready to appreciate the

brilliance of the final utterances. I am glad to have been able to soak myself in this noble material and to have had the energy to put my conclusions into a book. The wonder of a man who, in spite of an almost total lack of formal schooling, could produce eloquence which will be appreciated as long as English is spoken, grows upon me.

The title of the Lincoln book, like so many of the others, came with difficulty. To speak of Lincoln simply as a theologian seemed inadequate and possibly misleading, but how else could it be said? He was indeed a theologian because he had a genuine knowledge of God, but something more was needed. Then in May 1972, while conferring in London with Melvin Arnold, the Harper representative, we spoke of the contemporary agony, and the title came. Suddenly, I saw that it was out of the anguish of the divided country that the fundamental insights of Lincoln arose. I realized that we have both division and anguish in our own generation, and that ideas developed more than a century ago may be pertinent now. Accordingly, I decided to use as a title *Abraham Lincoln: Theologian of American Anguish,* and I have been happy about the particular choice of words. With the title finally selected, I came home and started writing. It has brought to my career as an author a kind of climax.

5. Minister

The bit of the road that most requires to be illuminated
is the point where it forks.

John Baillie

In my college journal I wrote one day that I was trying to decide
whether I should be a professor, an author, or a minister. Fortunately, it was never necessary to make that decision because in
actual experience the three vocations, instead of being mutually
exclusive, turned out to require one another. Therefore, there is
a sense in which for fifty years I have been engaged in the
Christian ministry. The fact that I chose not to be the pastor
of a church did not mean that I had rejected the ministry—far
from it.

My engagement in the ministry has been a natural result of
my participation in the Quaker heritage. There is, so far as I
know, no Christian body in which the ministry has been empha-
sized as much as in the Religious Society of Friends. "It is a
living ministry," wrote William Penn, "that begets a living
people; and by a living ministry at first we were reached and
turned to the Truth." Friends began very early to think of the
ministry in two different but not inconsistent ways. In one sense,
it was maintained, all Christians are called to the ministry re-

gardless of their particular secular occupations. In another sense, however, Friends were sufficiently realistic to see that some are much better adapted to a public ministry than is generally the case. It was expected that men of the character of George Fox and William Penn would speak on all occasions, and in that the people were not disappointed.

One of the earliest and clearest statements of that important distinction was made by Robert Barclay. "We do believe and affirm," he wrote, "that some are more particularly called to the work of the ministry, and therefore are fitted of the Lord for that purpose; whose work is more constantly and particularly to instruct, exhort, admonish, oversee, and watch over their brethren; and that . . . there is something more incumbent upon them in that respect than upon every common believer." Accepting the realism of Barclay, early Friends soon began to keep an approved list of those who appeared to be called to the ministry in a public sense. It was solemnly recorded that certain persons were to be accepted, wherever they might go, as ministers of the gospel. In accordance with that practice, I was recorded as a minister in New England Yearly Meeting of Friends on May 12, 1923.

In the fifty years which have followed, the concept of the ministry has affected me deeply. I have tried to judge every assignment, whether academic, literary, or governmental, by the standard of the ministry to which I am dedicated. Will this position, I have often asked myself when an offer has been made, be consistent with the practice of the ministry in its deepest sense? By this standard some options obviously have to be rejected, but these are not the difficult ones. What is really difficult is to distinguish between degrees of effective ministry in the world. Such a question was uppermost in my mind in two extremely difficult decisions in my career, the decision to go to Stanford in 1936, and the decision to go to Earlham in 1946. The significance of the ministerial criterion is especially clear in the fork of the road which appeared in 1946. Why should I join

Tom Jones in the Earlham experiment? To do so meant less income and far less academic prestige. To join a small and relatively unknown college would not help me in the American Philosophical Association or in the general teaching fraternity. Some of my Stanford colleagues were plainly shocked, partly because they did not even know where Earlham College was.

On purely academic grounds the 1946 decision was absurd. For one thing, I was giving up security because there was no certainty that the dream would materialize. The decision made sense by only one criterion, that of devotion to the ministry. It turned out to be a crucial difference. At Stanford University, of course, I had, in the very fact that I was chaplain as well as professor, abundant opportunities in the ministry as ordinarily understood. I had preaching responsibilities as well as teaching ones, and also every freedom to build small disciplined groups. Many persons, especially alumni, turned to the Memorial Church when they contemplated marriage or when they faced death in their families, and those instances often permitted me to minister to persons at their times of maximum openness. In honesty, I had to admit that however much I valued my relationship to the students in my classes, it was through the religious aspect of my university work that I was chiefly known. Though I tried to change the image, there were many who looked upon me as a clergyman. That irked me, but it was a battle which I could never wholly win. Though I never told them so, I was always embarrassed when a few of my colleagues called me "Padre," for my self-image was a radically different one.

At Stanford at the center of the campus there was a magnificent place of worship, but at Earlham in 1946 there was none. Some of the money which came from Earlham Hall, Norwich, England, on the death of Joseph John Gurney in 1847 had been intended for the construction of a meetinghouse, but the financial strain of those days required that all available funds should be used for academic purposes. With the new surge of vigor after the war, we began to talk at once of the wisdom of trying to build a meetinghouse. Even before we had secured the money, we knew something of the style in which we hoped the building would be built, all of us favoring the early American simplicity. I told President Jones that I was willing to undertake the task of raising the necessary funds because I deeply believed in the project. We needed one big gift, and it came from the children of John and Adaline Stout, Charles Stout of Memphis being the chief donor.

In our effort to combine intellectual and spiritual vitality, the building of the place of worship was an asset of incalculable worth, particularly because the sharing was so widespread. More than five hundred men and women, and even children, worked on the building for about a year, the labor of volunteers being directed by a skilled construction manager. The local labor unions expressed their agreement with the arrangement. Students laid all of the stone in the three porch areas, the stone itself being a gift from a company located near Bedford, Indiana. Most of the polishing of the exposed beams was done by staff members. All of the benches in the large meeting room were constructed and assembled on location, and they were deliberately left mobile, a feature which makes it possible to use the room for a variety of purposes. Normally, in worship, the benches are arranged in a hollow square, with no altar, pulpit, or other focus of attention on the part of the worshipers.

We estimated that we saved almost a hundred thousand dollars by the use of five hundred unpaid volunteers, who worked along with some professional help, but it was not the financial saving that we prized most. What made the greatest difference in the long run was the sense of being members of a community of people who worked together for an unselfish purpose. They were not merely constructing a building; they were, by their labor, providing a practical embodiment of their vision of wholeness.

One of the enjoyable aspects of the meetinghouse project, so far as I was concerned, was the connection with English donors. When, following the death of Rufus Jones in 1948, I first corresponded with Mrs. Arthur Eddington of Norwich, I learned that the old meetinghouse at Wymondham, where the young Gurneys had worshiped, was being dismantled, and that part of it might be available for transportation to America. By means of visits to East Anglia in both 1948 and 1950, the transfer of ownership was accomplished. The ancient benches from Wymondham were installed in our new Quiet Room, and tiles from the same place provided hearths for all three fireplaces. An oak beam, now more than two hundred years old, adorns the fireplace in the central room, which is, accordingly, named the Wymondham Room. The library, named for Alvin T. and Evelyn M. Coate of Indianapolis, and the day nursery, named for Pauline Trueblood, are features which we have come to value greatly.

The Stout Memorial Meetinghouse is a splendid demonstration of how deeds and words can be combined in creative fashion. It is indeed the scene of many words, as well as much corporate silence, but always in the background is the joy of having worked with our own hands. Also, the visible evidence of the historical connections with England has been elevating. After the Friends of Norwich had donated the valuable Wymondham mementos, the contemporary Gurneys decided to contribute paintings of both Joseph John Gurney, the spiritual founder of Earlham College, and his famous sister, Elizabeth Fry. These hang now in the Wymondham Room where they are seen by many. One feature which even the casual visitor cannot miss is the old and well-used ox-yoke over the central fireplace. For all who understand, it is a reminder, more potent than mere words, of Christ's call to commitment.

Soon after entering upon my Earlham duties I realized that the new undertaking might combine, almost perfectly, my three vocations of teaching, of writing, and of ministering. Fortunately, this is the way it has turned out to be. Freedom from teaching half of each academic year gave time for me to pursue my public ministry in various parts of the nation. In some years I spoke in a different city almost every Sunday, enjoying a freedom which I had not known for a long time. I welcomed the regular invitations to the Chicago Sunday Evening Club, in Orchestra Hall, to Sage Chapel, Cornell University, and to many other places. Frequently, I preached in some village church in Ohio or Indiana, an experience I valued regardless of denominational affiliations.

As the pattern of my life became established after our removal to Indiana, I gave more and more of my time to the traveling ministry. A small portion of that ministry was carried on during the semester I devoted to teaching, but my outside engagements were usually limited during those periods. The theory was that I could be most productive if I devoted one-third of each year to teaching, one-third to speaking, and one-third to writing. Most of the traveling ministry thus occurred from February 1 to June 1. Invitations were accepted, not on the basis of geography, but rather in the light of potential effectiveness.

More and more the engagement which includes a series of four days in one town, one college, or one church has seemed more valuable than the single address. The ideal arrangement, tried out in many parts of the country, is that in which I speak twice each day, Sunday through Wednesday. The Sunday beginning gives impetus at the start, and often this continues to the end. The weekday evening sessions are naturally better attended than are the morning ones, but the addresses in the mornings can profitably be devoted to specialized topics. Some of these may be frankly educational, dealing with Biblical and theological themes. Now, in my retirement, I am finding it possible to extend the time assigned to one place and to give a week or more as "theologian in residence." Much future ministry in the churches may reasonably be of this type. The local congregation or group of congregations thus becomes, at least temporarily, a lay academy.

Though the Religious Society of Friends has provided me with a base, my field has not been limited by sectarian considerations. In short, I believe in ecumenicity, and have seriously tried to practice it. I have said in many sermons that while I do not know how big Christ's Church is, I at least know that it is bigger than my own. It gave me both surprise and delight when I was invited to preach from a Roman Catholic pulpit in Connecticut and to share in the leadership of retreats in Franciscan Centers in both Florida and Arizona.

One of my most prized opportunities in the ecumenical ministry came in the late summer of 1948. The Friends Yearly Meeting was held that year at Edinburgh, largely in honor of Robert Barclay, who had been born in Scotland three hundred years earlier. I gave the Barclay Tercentenary Lecture in the Assembly Hall of the Church of Scotland, and many Presbyterians, including John Baillie, attended. From Edinburgh I went, accompanied by two other Quakers, Howard Brinton and Thomas Brown, to the Island of Iona because we were attracted by the dream so persuasively expressed by George MacLeod. All of my subsequent ministry has been influenced by the few days which we spent on the famous island.

From Iona I traveled to Amsterdam, where I represented Friends in the formative Assembly of the World Council of Churches. I was lodged in the little hotel occupied by the devoted brothers, Donald and John Baillie. Another occupant was Richard Raines, later to be Methodist Bishop of Indiana. When Donald Baillie's book *God Was in Christ* was published, I felt a special tenderness for the author who, as a respected professor at St. Andrews, maintained a warm evangelical faith with no sense of embarrassment. The men with whom I shared breakfast daily in August 1948 affected my own ministry more than they realized. Increasingly, my prayer was that I might be able to combine the warm heart and the clear head.

The Assembly at Amsterdam was a truly impressive occasion. No one who was present can forget the day when the Archbishop of Canterbury stood upon the platform of the Concertgebau and said, "Now, for the first time in history, the World Council of Churches is in being." The most moving features of the Assembly, for many of us, were the periods of worship arranged each morning. By the surprising genius of someone in the Geneva office, each of them was different, and each represented the best that a particular constituent group could offer. Thus one morning we followed the order of Morning Prayer of the Anglican communion; on another, a Lutheran service; and so on throughout the week. In that manner we demonstrated, not uniformity, but the profound idea of unity in difference. The resultant effect was like the beauty of the patchwork quilt, rather than that of the dull gray blanket. We were observing the new ecumenicity in practice!

On Saturday morning it was desired that Quakers should offer the best that they could give. Because I was at that time chairman of the Friends World Committee for Consultation, the Geneva office asked me to be in charge. It was obvious that the best Quaker contribution is the unique development according to which, whatever preparation of mind and spirit the worshipers may have had before assembling, the actual time of worship is one in which each seeks to be both open and obedient to the leadership of the Spirit. We decided to engage in that venture, even though we recognized that for the majority of those present the experience would be wholly new and strange.

On the morning assigned to that spiritual experiment about six hundred persons assembled and found seats in the many-sided Koepelkerk. Though technically I was in charge, I elected not to enter the high pulpit, but to sit on one of the regular benches accompanied by Howard Brinton and a few other

Friends. Early in the summer the Geneva office had written to me at Richmond, asking me to provide an order of worship which could be distributed in the pews. I answered that there would be no order of worship, but that I would gladly write a statement of explanation which I hoped would be helpful to people as they should enter the place of worship. The statement, which I wrote and which was printed in three languages, German, French, and English, explained that the time of worship would be wholly under the guidance of the Holy Spirit. I added that there were two ways in which attenders could harm it if they wished. One way, I said, was the advance decision to speak; the other was the advance decision to remain silent! The only way, consequently, in which anyone could help was by the advance decision to be obedient. In the final phrasing I was influenced by Thomas Kelly whom we had already lost, and who had coined the term "Holy Obedience."

The Amsterdam meeting for worship was a powerful one from every point of view. We had silence, but we also had vocal prayers in both French and German, as well as effective brief messages in English. One of the best messages was that of Dr. W. A. Visser 't Hooft, then general secretary of the World Council, who, like myself, was a former Woodbrooker. At the end of the time allotted I asked the attenders to postpone casual conversation until they were outside the building, and to my satisfaction I did not hear one word as we walked out into the sunshine. We had experienced the ecumenicity in which each group shares what it has to offer, and each is willing to learn from the others.

At the beginning of 1950, in the exact middle of our century, a remarkable occasion occurred at Rock Island, Illinois, sponsored by the Inter-seminary Movement and attended chiefly by young men. It was good to attend the gathering and to feel the new pulse of spiritual vitality then appearing. The most memorable address was that of Bishop Stephen Neill, one of the leading

Christian statesmen of our century, who, though an Anglican, really belongs to all Christians. From his lips I heard at Rock Island for the first time in my life the phrase "the equipping ministry." The phrase may have been employed before, but if so, I do not know when or where. In any case, Bishop Neill made an impact that day which has extended to the entire Christian community. We realized instantly, as we heard his fresh interpretation of Ephesians 4:12, that we were listening to a conception which can give unity to all of the ministry in which we are engaged.

The central idea of the new emphasis is that the characteristic Christian ministry is that of enabling other people in their ministry, and equipping them to perform it. When later I read the clear translation of Ephesians in *The New English Bible,* I was humbled in that I had not seen the revolutionary significance of the passage earlier. The purpose of God's gifts to pastors and teachers, we are told, is "to equip God's people for work in his service." This means that if a person is a Christian at all, he has to be, in some sense, a minister, but he is not likely to be fully effective in his ministry unless there are some persons who are dedicated to its guidance and enrichment.

If my vocation was to equip, what should be my particular emphasis in doing so? My effort to answer that practical question is reflected in many of the journal entries in my notebook of that period of my life. I was soon convinced that though I might have many different tasks to perform, some of them humble ones, the central ministry which I could perform, and ought to perform, was that of intellectual clarification. I became increasingly conscious of the vast amount of confusion in the family of man. I saw that millions of people, including a good many church members, do not really believe anything at all and consequently have no firm center in their lives. More and more I turned to the revealing passage in Matthew 9:35–38, about the confusion of the crowds, linking it with Christ's call to commitment in the famous yoke passage, Matthew 11:28–30, and recognizing that the latter is more understandable if it is seen as an answer to the former.

The more I looked at Christ's key words in Matthew 9:36 the more obvious was their contemporary ring. "When he saw the crowds, he had compassion for them, because they were harassed and helpless, like sheep without a shepherd" are words that can be employed today with no alteration of any kind. As I meditated, I realized that meaninglessness is the worst thing that can happen to human beings. The human creature, because he is very hardy, can bear various kinds of suffering, including poverty and pain, but he cannot bear meaninglessness very long. Unless someone comes to his rescue, he goes to pieces, and this is true regardless of affluence or lack of it. But who will help or can help? It is in this connection that "the harvest is plentiful, but the laborers are few" (Matthew 9:37, Luke 10:2).

When I had reached the point just mentioned, the right emphasis of my own ministry became clearer. Both my training and my temperament prepared me to help people in their own thinking. I saw that there is a crying need for Christian intellectuals and that some effort must be made to equip those who are fitted to perform such a calling. Without neglecting emotion, I knew that feeling is far from sufficient and that consequently the Christian, if he is to be effective in our confused world, must love God with all his mind.

At about that time I also recognized that we are at a stage in which, since addition will not suffice, we must have multiplication. Accordingly, I began about 1950 to select my speaking opportunities in the light of what I called "Operation Multiplication." Where a choice could be made, I often spoke to groups of pastors rather than to undifferentiated public assemblages. I did that, not because I thought pastors are better persons than others, which they may not be, but rather because they are peculiarly placed where, if they have something to give, they can make a crucial difference. More and more I sought to equip the equippers, hoping that the books which I was writing might become tools in the hands of some who were attempting to prepare others for their own ministry. Whenever I hear that something which I have produced laboriously has been used in the public ministry of others, I am glad, for, if anything is worth saying, it is worth repeating.

That particular conception of Christian strategy led me to accept, on three occasions, an attractive invitation to serve Wesley Seminary in Washington, D.C. In each case my wife and I stayed at the seminary for a two-week period, living with the students and being available to them every day. Though I spoke in the chapel and taught a few classes, the important impact came in the meetings of small spontaneously gathered groups of young men and in private conversations. The value of the meetings has been verified by subsequent friendships with the same persons, most of whom are now active pastors. What helped most was that each young man, struggling to see his right place in the ministry, had a chance to talk with someone who had no academic or ecclesiastic authority over him. Accordingly, each could talk freely.

The repeated Wesley connection brought happy relationships with several older people, especially President and Mrs. Norman Trott, and Dr. and Mrs. Luther Neff. Recently, we have been able to visit the Neffs in the Manor House at Seaford, Delaware. Another prized contact during the Wesley visits was that with Edith Hamilton. We visited her in her beautiful home on Massachusetts Avenue and found the ninety-four-year-old woman reading galley proof of her introductions to the *Dialogues of Plato*, later published in the Bollingen Series. I had met Miss Hamilton earlier on shipboard and considered her one of the finest of contemporary writers of English prose. In spite of her advanced age, she was planning, when we saw her, to take a summer tour in Germany.

One of our most enjoyable experiments in the ministry to academia was a short course carried on at St. Andrews College, Laurinburg, North Carolina, with the encouragement and support of President Ansley Moore. The plan was to give the college three weeks one winter, with lectures each Tuesday and Thursday evening, and with numerous personal contacts each day. We assembled a class of two hundred people, one hundred being recruited from the student body and another hundred made up of people from surrounding towns. An effort was made to draw the attention of students, regardless of age, to the really great books, including those written by undoubted Christian intellectuals, and more than two hundred were sold. The value of the extended period in one place is hard to overestimate. I saw that the traveling ministry is multiplied in its effectiveness if it abjures the strategy of hit and run.

The decision to give several days in one place led naturally to the acceptance of invitations to conference centers. I have spoken many times in recent years at Lake Chautauqua, New York. Several of my books have been presented first, in oral form, in the Chautauqua Hall of Philosophy, and frequently I have given the Sunday morning sermon in the auditorium. Other valued opportunities have been provided by Massanetta Springs, Virginia, and both Montreat and Lake Junaluska in the North Carolina mountains. I have found that the people who gather in such places are unusually receptive.

As I meditated more and more on the particular calling of Christian intellectuals, to which Edith Hamilton was so obviously dedicated, I realized that we need to rethink our approach to academic communities. The common approach to these in the recent past has been woefully ineffective largely because it has been directed to the wrong problem. When Christianity is demoted to the dispensing of soft drinks and the organization of recreation, the salt has already lost its savor. What is needed on every campus is the deliberate formation of cadres of able minds, primarily on the professorial level, ready to accept the challenge of the surrounding and now seemingly dominant paganism. When I come into contact with a competent biologist or historian or economist who is at the same time and without compartmentalization an unapologetic Christian, I thank God. Such a person may be effective precisely because he works within the academic system, rather than pecking at the edges. The more such persons can be recruited and equipped, the better for our culture. An encouraging recent development is that at Purdue University where Ian Barbour occupies the new Chair of Science and Theology. Though the Christian faith can use people of modest endowment, in the long run it cannot become a truly redemptive force in the total culture until it has, in its service, the best minds. Because the recruitment of good minds has occurred in many past generations, there is no reason to suppose that it is impossible in our own.

Though I was never privileged to meet C. S. Lewis, his influence on me has been greater than I at first realized. When, after the death of Lewis, I enjoyed a productive conversation with Dr. J. B. Phillips, I found that though Dr. Phillips had never met Lewis either, our conversation turned to him almost at once. The influence of many persons fades rapidly at their death, but C. S. Lewis is now appreciated even more than he was while he was among the living. The words which he wrote with such power of thought are even more convincing today. We still have some academicians who assert blandly that belief in the existence of God is now obsolete, or that what they vulgarly call "God-language" is no longer relevant, but their intellectual position is made extremely difficult if they have the courage to face the careful reasoning of Lewis. What we need desperately is many more like him. Our hope lies in the emergence of Christian intellectuals who are able to meet the double requirement of competence in some particular field of inquiry, whether it be physics or psychology or some other, and also a firm grounding in Christian truth.

No vital Christianity is possible unless at least three aspects of it are developed. These three are the inner life of devotion, the outer life of service, and the intellectual life of rationality. In short, the Christian is called, not to just one operation, but to three. In different periods of human history the need of emphasis among these three has varied, depending upon which one of them has been the object of relative neglect. When the social gospel was first inaugurated, for example, it was the service aspect which had been neglected. There is little doubt which operation needs emphasis now; it is the third one. We have experienced a woeful failure to support the credibility of the gospel, some leaders even asserting that there is no need of it. By settling for faith alone, they seem to avoid the necessity of thinking, but the sorrowful fact is that when this route is followed, there is no way left to distinguish between false and true faiths. As I began to see that the heart of my own ministry lay in the attempt to help balance a distortion, I turned more and more to the golden text of all Christian intellectuals, "Always be prepared to make a defense to any one who calls you to account for the hope that is in you, yet do it with gentleness and reverence" (I Peter 3:15).

Since the purpose of this book is to record as faithfully as possible the various steps of my personal pilgrimage, I need to try to recount something of how my emphasis has changed with the years. "The great thing to be recorded," said Dr. Johnson in reference to autobiographical writing, "is the state of your own mind." In trying to report faithfully in this regard I have the advantage of notations which are preserved in diaries and journals in which I have written off and on for fully fifty years. Because these are interesting to me, I feel they may interest my readers.

In the early days of my ministry I believed in God and undoubtedly thought of myself as a Christian, but my theology was not evangelical. Though in my spoken ministry I often mentioned Christ, I did not emphasize His uniqueness. I spoke much of His compassion, of His emphasis upon love of the brethren, and of His faith in men, demonstrated by His recruitment of such unlikely specimens of humanity as the Twelve Apostles, but I tended to omit His teaching about Himself and His unique relation to the Father.

Subtly and slowly the change in my message began to appear. The influences were of course numerous, but it may have been the writings of C. S. Lewis that first shocked me out of my unexamined liberalism. In reading Lewis I could not escape the conclusion that the popular view of Christ as being a Teacher, and *only* a Teacher, has within it a self-contradiction that cannot be resolved. I saw, in short, that conventional liberalism cannot survive rigorous and rational analysis. What Lewis and a few others made me face was the hard fact that if Christ was only a Teacher, then He was a false one, since, in His teaching, He claimed to be *more*. The supposition that He taught only, or even chiefly, about loving one another is simply not true. The hard fact is that if Christ was not in a unique sense "the image of the invisible God" (Colossians 1:15), as the early Christians believed, then He was certainly the arch impostor and charlatan of history.

C. S. Lewis reached me primarily because he turned the intellectual tables. I was wholly accustomed to a world in which the sophisticates engaged in attack, while the Christians sought bravely to be on the defense, but Lewis turned this around and forced the unbeliever into a posture of defense. In the *Screwtape Letters* dated July 5, 1941, at Magdalen College, Oxford, Lewis, who up to that time had been an inconspicuous academician, inaugurated a new Christian strategy. I had already begun to sense that however vulnerable the Christian position may be, the position of the opposition is more vulnerable still. Once when a graduate student asked one of my professors whether the study of philosophy would help him in the support of the Christian faith, the professor replied, "No, it will not; but it will do something else of great importance—it will help you to see the weaknesses of the enemies of the faith."

The first of the weapons employed by Lewis as he began to establish a new style of dialogue was humor, a weapon then sorely needed. He had noted the striking advice of Martin Luther, "The best way to drive out the devil, if he will not yield to texts of Scripture, is to jeer and flout him, for he cannot bear scorn." In the pre-Lewis days many supposed, uncritically, that the opponents of Christianity had a monopoly upon reason, while the Christian had nothing to rely upon except faith. Lewis, to the delight of his many readers, reversed that assumption, adopting an approach reminiscent of that initiated by G. K. Chesterton. Screwtape, the arch Devil, in advising his nephew about the handling of a person who is weakening in his atheism, and is even somewhat attracted to Christ, tells him that above all he dare not let the fellow *think.* If he thinks, says Screwtape, he will be lost to *us.*

Though Lewis helped me in many ways, he helped me most by making me face the teaching of Christ in its wholeness. If in *Screwtape* he taught me to watch for the irrationality of the opposition, it was in *The Case for Christianity* (1943) that he became unanswerable. When I first read the crucial paragraph about Christ as Teacher, it struck me with great force, partly because I had begun already to be skeptical about the conventional liberalism of my student days. In short, though I felt that something was wrong, it took a man of the intellectual straightforwardness of Lewis to make me see it definitely and clearly. What I saw in 1943, and have seen ever since, is that the Good Teacher conception is one option which Christ does not allow us to take. We can reject Him; we can accept Him on His terms; we cannot, with intellectual honesty, impose our own terms. The crucial paragraph is as follows:

> A man who was merely a man and said the sort of things Jesus said would not be a great moral teacher. He would either be a

lunatic—on a level with the man who says he is a poached egg —or else he would be the Devil of Hell. You must make your choice. Either this man was, and is, the Son of God: or else a madman or something worse. You can shut Him up for a fool, you can spit at Him and kill Him as a demon; or you can fall at His feet and call Him Lord and God. But let us not come with any patronizing nonsense about His being a great human teacher. He has not left that open to us. He did not intend to.

With that tremendous challenge in my consciousness I began to look at the Gospels in a new light. What *did* Christ say about Himself and His unique relation to the Father? I could of course minimize His reported teaching in John's Gospel on the hypothesis that the words reported there are a reflection of later teaching. Thus when I read "No one comes to the Father, but by me" or "He who has seen me has seen the Father" (John 14:6, 9), I could reply that those clear statements may not have been the actual utterances of Christ, but I could not employ that argument when I dealt with the Synoptics and particularly with that strand in them which, according to the best scholarship, is part of the original material on which the Synoptic authors drew. No part of Christ's teaching has greater evidence of authenticity than that which, evidently drawn from the same source, appears in Matthew 11:27 and Luke 10:22, "All things have been delivered to me by my Father; and no one knows the Son except the Father, and no one knows the Father except the Son and any one to whom the Son chooses to reveal him."

New strength came into my ministry both public and private when I saw that either I had to reject Christ and the admiring talk, or accept Him on His own terms. As though illumined by a great light, I saw that He did not ask for admiration; He asked for commitment! To the perplexed, the confused, the distraught, He said and still says "Come to me." In all the relativities of this world there is, if Christ is right, one solid place. He offers "rest," not in the sense of passivity, but in that of a place to stand, a center of trustworthiness in the midst of the world's confusion. When I suddenly realized that my one central certainty was the trustworthiness of Christ, my preaching took on a new note of confidence, which I tried to convey to others. Thus I began to emphasize, in a new context, the concept of trustworthiness. This word had appeared in the title of my Swarthmore Lecture, given in London in May 1939 and published by Allen and Unwin as *The Trustworthiness of Religious Experience*. I kept the term, but applied it in a unique way to Jesus Christ. Without intending to do so, I had become an evangelical Christian. I found that instead of being embarrassed by them any more, as many of my associates were, I could sing with joy and full intellectual acceptance the much loved gospel hymns such as "Jesus, Lover of My Soul" and "My Faith Looks Up to Thee."

New confidence in Christ provided me with a rational answer to a number of important questions. I had of course long believed in God, and I had recognized the force of the cumulative evidence for theism, but now I had a new approach. With Christ as my center of certitude, I was driven inevitably to God because Christ believed in Him! The logic was sharp and clear: either God is, or Christ was wrong. I found that such reasoning could be made clear to "average" people who made no claims to intellectual competence.

What emerged was a new theological approach. I discovered that when I spoke of God, people were polite but unimpressed, partly because so much of the sharpness of meaning had been eroded by talk of God as an impersonal Force. It was obvious that no thoughtful person would be greatly interested in a Power so abstract as the law of gravity. At least one kind of agnosticism can be maintained with integrity, but it is something about which no one ever becomes excited. In reading Gabriel Marcel I recognized what he meant when he spoke of "the system of values ultimately bound up with the desert in which I was expected to live." If God is, but is not a Person, ours is a desert universe indeed.

The new strategy, which influenced my ministry, was to move, not from God to Christ, but from Christ to God. Thereby we start in our epistemological pilgrimage at the point of most reasonable assurance. If Christ is trustworthy, it follows that God really and objectively *is*, for Christ prayed to Him in a completely personal way. What we experience is that which Martin Buber has taught us to call the "I-Thou" relationship. With awe and wonder I considered the tremendous significance of the prayer of Christ which appears in Matthew 11:25 and Luke 10:21, "I thank thee, Father, Lord of heaven and earth, that thou hast hidden these things from the wise and understanding and revealed them to babes." In that one prayer I began to see an entire theology by which people can live and which is compatible with the strictest rationality.

When I found that thoughtful people would listen to a Christ-centered approach, I realized where the power of the Christian faith resides. While many churches are declining in strength, the churches which exhibit both Christ-centeredness and rationality are marked by evident vitality. A natural consequence of this fruitful combination is devotion to justice and a real concern for persons. Once a ministry accepts unapologetically the conviction of the Christlikeness of God, we have a firm launching pad from which we can operate with confidence and make a consequent difference in the world.

6. Yokefellow

> The supreme wonder of the history of the Christian Church is that always in the moments when it has seemed most dead, out of its own body there has sprung up new life.
>
> William Temple

As I came into middle age, two separate dangers were simultaneously impressed upon my mind. I saw, at the same time, both the futility of empty freedom and the fruitlessness of single effort. Affirmatively stated, the latter led to the idea of the small fellowship, while the former led to the idea of voluntary discipline; in conjunction they led to the recognition that hope lies in the creation of an order. Now, for a quarter of a century, much of my thought and energy have been employed in both the dream and its embodiment in one particular order, the Order of the Yoke.

The conviction that in the promotion of the Christian Cause a new approach is needed, was deeply impressed upon me in my final years as chaplain of Stanford University. I began to see where the power is, and where it is not. I observed among our soldier students the obvious strength of the Orthodox Jews with whom I met in the vestry of Memorial Church on Friday evenings. Their cohesiveness and their personal discipline were two sides of the same pattern of living. In contrast to the attendance at a conventional student gathering, which was always unpredictable, the attendance of Orthodox Jews on Friday nights sometimes amounted to 100 percent of those involved. They were faithful and they were participants largely because they had a rule by which they undertook to live. Suddenly I saw that those young men, though they were not Christians, exhibited some of the characteristics of the Christian orders about which I had read with both interest and admiration.

The spiritual growth at Stanford in 1945 was the consequence of small committed and disciplined groups. Beginning with one group which met in the chapel for prayer every noon, the movement grew until there were such groups in every living unit throughout the entire campus. The Chapel Cabinet was remodeled into a group which included prayer as well as discussion and action, and in which each member began to accept a serious discipline of the interior life. Without conscious intention, something of the character of an order was actually emerging.

During those days I thought a great deal of what orders had meant in the history of the Christian faith, especially after I read the life of St. Francis by G. K. Chesterton. Much as I admired the work of the First Order and the Second Order of St. Francis, I admired the Third Order most because it was envisioned as a way of meeting the needs of those who were involved in common life. At Stanford the idea was so infectious that some of the members of the Chapel Cabinet began calling themselves "tertiaries." We were convinced that far from needing any new denominations, we may actually be entering the post-denominational age. We knew that whereas denominations have existed for only about four hundred years, orders have existed far longer. The effectiveness of the Benedictine Order, especially in the penetration of pagan England, is impressive to anyone who knows the story. Perhaps, we said, we require contemporary orders, developed in our own century; we need not, we said, depend wholly upon former patterns because new ones can emerge now.

When we referred to an order, we meant something radically different from a denomination; we envisioned a horizontal fellowship, cutting across existing religious lines. The new grouping, we thought, would not supplant the existing churches nor work against them, but would rather work *within* them for the purpose of renewal. We saw that our deepest fellowships, far from being limited to our own denominations, tend to transcend them, some of our best friendships being with those who are members of bodies other than our own. That indeed is part of what is meant in calling ours a post-denominational age, though emphatically it need not be a post-Christian age. The members of the emerging order, we saw, are marked both by the intensity of their fellowship and by their spiritual self-discipline. Instead of being permissive with themselves, they are tough, and in spite of their failures, they have a rule by which they seek to live. Such a rule naturally is very different from that of any medieval order in that it is one appropriate to life in the modern world. The new rule which must be developed, far from being geared to life in a monastery, is one made by and for men and women who, because they have children to rear, taxes to pay, and work to do, cannot be cloistered.

With that kind of thinking as a background, I moved to the Middle West in 1946 and almost at once began to discover that others were thinking similarly. In the winter of 1945, when I gave a series of lectures at McCormick Theological Seminary in Chicago on "The Idea of a Redemptive Society," I found a ready response among the students and professors. A few at McCormick began to meet regularly and to think of themselves as part of a developing order. In my first year at Earlham, 1946–1947, I met with a group of students for whom the dream began to make a real difference in their personal lives, though their fellowship had as yet no name. That is why, when I wrote

Alternative to Futility in the summer of 1947, I dedicated the book as follows: "To those students of Earlham who have provided a demonstration, rather than an argument, in support of the theme of this book."

The new groups which began about the middle of the century to appear across the country were known by a variety of names, some of them being called "cell groups," though nobody was really satisfied with the term. The earliest conferences of the scattered "cells" were those held on the campus of the University of Michigan at Ann Arbor under the leadership of Franklin Littell, then director of Lane Hall. In those earliest gatherings there was not enough emphasis upon either a disciplined order or a universal ministry, for, though the idea was growing, it was far removed from full development. The Inter-seminary Movement, particularly in its gathering at Miami University, Oxford, Ohio, went further in helping people to understand what a group can become.

Two important steps, so far as my own thinking was concerned, came in August 1948 and in May 1949. The former came in my visit to Iona, when I participated for the first time in the Iona Fellowship. I saw that under the inspiring leadership of George MacLeod, a new order had actually arisen, with the work of St. Columba as its model. At Iona I saw a developed pattern which included interior discipline, ministry, evangelism, and social action. The discipline of beginning each day with prayer, seeking to go through the day in prospect, and asking God's guidance upon each detail, appealed to me so mightily that I have sought ever since, not only to practice it myself, but also to lead others into it. The rhythm of withdrawal and encounter, basic to the Iona pattern of Christian vocation, is obviously sound. On Sunday, when I was present, the sermon delivered in the restored Cathedral of the Isles was entitled "The Mountain and the Plain," a message based upon Mark 9:2–29. The fact that Christ withdrew to the mountain retreat even while the people needed Him, and later returned to them in human service, was to me a fresh insight. I saw that such a rhythm must be an essential element of any new order worth developing in our generation.

The crucial experience came in May 1949, nine months after the visit to Iona. Having promised to preach on Sunday at the First Baptist Church of Cleveland, I traveled by Pullman train from Dayton so as to have a good night's rest and if possible to be alert on Sunday morning. After completing my sleep and a quiet breakfast in the Terminal Building, I boarded the Rapid Transit for Cleveland Heights. Already, under the influence of Frank Laubach, I had begun the practice of reading every morning from the New Testament, whatever my location might be. Instead of skipping about in the Scriptures, I had adopted the discipline of going straight through a book, reading slowly about eleven verses a day if the topic admitted of such a division, and noting, in the margin, the place and date of reading. This system of dating has come to be personally valuable in that my New Testament has in one sense become also my diary. Many different copies of the New Testament have now been dated in this fashion, and these become reminders of high moments in a quarter century.

My reading that morning on the Rapid Transit was Matthew 11:25–30. Though I had of course read the passage on many former occasions, it struck me then with unique force. It was almost as though I had never before read the words "Take my yoke upon you." Suddenly, I saw that this is Christ's clearest call to commitment. I realized that the yoke metaphor involves what we most require if the vitality of the Christian faith is to be recovered. Being yoked with Christ may mean a great deal more, but at least it means being a participant rather than a spectator; it also means accepting a discipline which leads paradoxically to a new kind of freedom; it leads finally to fellowship because the yokes which we know best cannot be worn alone. Within a minute or so, as an entire complex of thinking came together, I had a different sermon. In my briefcase was a sermon which I had prepared, but I have no idea what its subject was, for it was entirely supplanted by a new and exciting vision. The words which came to me on the train that morning I preached within the hour, recognizing that I was participating in a new development. Later, when I wrote as faithfully as I could what I had said that morning, it became the first chapter of the book *The Yoke of Christ.*

Suddenly, in 1949, we had a name for our hitherto nameless fellowship which was beginning to be a conscious one. We saw that the term "Yokefellow," which is employed in the New Testament (Philippians 4:3) as a synonym for a practicing Christian, derives its entire significance from the yoke passage on which I had felt led to speak at the First Baptist Church of Cleveland. The advantages of the term "Yokefellow" are obvious in that it is a Biblical term and is also free from the ambiguity of the word "cell." Furthermore, it provides a suitable nomenclature for the growing number of men and women who are unwilling to be known as either laymen or clergymen. Thus it appeared to be a genuine third way, and some grasped it eagerly. At the time that some of us began to employ the word "Yokefellow" we were not aware that it had been used in the nineteenth century, in essentially the same fashion, by Dwight L. Moody.

The first groups who picked up the name were those of McCormick Theological Seminary and the American Baptist Home Mission Society. Desiring a visible witness, Professor Vartan Melconian was the first to wear a pin in the shape of an ox-yoke, the original pin being carved from wild cherry wood at Warren Wilson College, Swannanoa, North Carolina. Professor Obert Tanner, who had been my associate at Stanford University, and who owned a jewelry manufacturing establishment in Salt Lake City, arranged for the production of gold pins appropriate for lapel wear, and the Baptists distributed them. Soon the pins began to appear in surprising places, so that people, who would otherwise have been strangers, began to feel that they belonged together. The greatest advantage of the use of the emblem is that in characteristic situations it has caused another person to inquire about its significance. The pin thereby becomes an occasion for a potentially effective witness of response.

Our major development after 1949 came in the winter and spring of 1951 because of a committed group of students at Earlham College. Returning from a long stay in England and feeling the need of a new start, I invited into our home one evening nine young men and women who seemed to me to be persons of unusual promise. One of them was Emily, a Christian student from Tokyo, who at the end of that year married a young pastor, Tetsuo Kobayashi, and soon became, along with her husband, an exponent of the Yokefellow idea in Japan. All of the others were of American families belonging to various denominations. I explained as best I could the possibility of a new kind of Christian fellowship which would include prayer, study, and human service. To each one I gave a copy of *Alternative to Futility,* asking each to read it and to come back on the following Tuesday evening if the idea appealed. If it did not appeal, I said, it was better to forget it entirely. I made the point that the message I had put into the book might be false, and it might be true, but it could not be *inconsequential.* The one option, I said, which is not available to an honest person is to say that the message is true and then do nothing about it. The urgency, I held, is intrinsic to the conception, rather than something added.

Most of the students came back the next week, bringing some others with them, and we were off to a great start. We loved one another; we thought together; we worked together in tasks of compassion. Within a few weeks the group was too large for its original purpose and we were forced to divide, recognizing the paradox that multiplication comes by division. Soon there were similar groups in other colleges, then in churches and later in factories. At our first regular meeting we worked on the creation of a minimum discipline, all recognizing that nothing of any importance is likely to survive without it. We knew that however valuable emotion may be, it can never of itself lead to endurance. Accordingly, we agreed upon a common discipline and printed a discipline card, which later in its use reached various parts of the world. The first card which we printed included only five disciplines: Daily Prayer, Daily Scripture, Weekly Worship, Proportionate Giving, and Study.

After a few months it began to dawn upon me that something was developing which was far beyond my capacity to handle alone. As the idea spread, the correspondence became heavy and I had no secretary. The lack of a secretary was one of the prices which I had paid in transferring from the affluence of Stanford to the relative poverty of Earlham. Requests for information and for assistance poured in both by post and by telephone, the requests indicating an almost pathetic hunger for a new kind of vitality which many admitted that they lacked, but believed to be possible. Though I was thrilled at the response, the burden was nevertheless real. Just when the burden began to seem intolerable, a new figure, Edward Gallahue, entered the scene. Mr. Gallahue, who was in the insurance business in Indianapolis, had wanted me to preach one Sunday in the local church to which he belonged, and I was able to comply. In his home, on Sunday afternoon, he asked about the new patterns which were beginning to appear in the Christian Cause and volunteered practical help. Learning that with no organization at all a new order was actually forming, he helped in two specific ways. First, he handed me a check, asking that I use it for secretarial assistance, postage, and printing. He said he believed that other men, if approached, would match him in that gesture and encouraged me to try to recruit them. Second, he proposed that while continuing to minimize organization, we should draw several men into a cabinet in order to provide counsel and spiritual support as well as financial backing. The group recruited for these purposes early in 1952 was the prototype of what finally became the governing board of Yokefellows International.

Increasingly, as I had felt the need of a group devoted to mutual support, the conviction had grown upon me that the isolated individual makes very little difference in the world. The voice crying in the wilderness is not remembered or even heard. "It is impossible," said John Baillie, "for men to meet with God and love Him without at the same time meeting with and loving one another." Recognizing the truth of Baillie's words, I felt keenly the need of being a part of a fellowship which would be small enough for the members to know one another and large enough to be truly effective. That fellowship I found at last in the men who began to meet in my home. When I look back now on the events of 1952 and consider the nature of that little galaxy, I am filled with amazement.

First there was Edward Gallahue, the businessman who, though both an intellectual and a sophisticate, was also, in his enthusiasm, unusually childlike. He cared greatly about mental health, his interest having been stimulated by the illness of his own mother. He became a friend of the Doctors Menninger and one of the most generous supporters of their clinic at Topeka, Kansas. Being drawn to Christianity largely on intellectual grounds, he recognized that since he could not be a Christian alone, he should, for the first time in his life, join a local church. After analyzing the values represented in many others, he decided that he could serve best as a Methodist. He lived long enough to put together in a book, *Edward's Odyssey*, the account of his spiritual pilgrimage. After months of pain, he died in July 1971.

A second member of that remarkable pioneer group was Dr.

H. V. Scott, a dedicated pediatrician living in Fort Wayne. The first meeting between Dr. Scott and me came in February 1951 when, after I had made an address in his city, he asked me a question. Sensing that his interest was not perfunctory, I arranged for an immediate and unhurried conference, and we have walked together ever since. He formed the first Yokefellow group to be made up wholly of physicians. When the Stout Memorial Meetinghouse was opened for use at Earlham College in April 1952, it was Dr. Scott who presented the attractive ox-yoke which now hangs above the mantel in the Wymondham Room. Fortunately, the new life represented by the beautiful meetinghouse and by the Yokefellow Movement emerged almost simultaneously. It was appropriate for Dr. Scott to become the first chairman of the board of Yokefellows International, a position he still holds.

A third member of that gathered fellowship was Robert Greenleaf, long associated in personnel training with the American Telephone and Telegraph Company. The idea of the yoke, with its emphasis upon the ministry in common life, appealed to him as both fresh and valid. A similar reaction was that of Harold Belt, an officer of the Fred Harvey Corporation and a member of Chicago's Central Church. His outstanding gift was, and is, his ability to stimulate others. In retirement, Mr. Belt is committed to the hope of making America's bicentennial celebration a time of spiritual reaffirmation.

Paul Davis, a man of the same type as those just mentioned, had earned, first at Stanford and then at Columbia, a national reputation in the field of university development. He knew how to raise money, not by asking for it directly, but by encouraging commitment to a vision. Understanding perfectly why it is fruitless to make small plans, he dreamed big dreams. Like Mr. Greenleaf, he is a Quaker, but the interests of neither man have ever been limited by the erection of sectarian fences.

William McKay, a wholesale grocer of Fort Wayne, originated the first adult Yokefellow group in our century, the fellowship arising out of tragedy and pain. When Mr. McKay's daughter was stricken with polio, several men, including Mr. McKay's pastor, John Meister, began meeting regularly in order to pray for the one who was ill. The project, as might reasonably have been expected, went far beyond the original purpose and has been the means of influencing numerous lives. Desiring to help others while they helped themselves, Mr. McKay's group undertook to make one of the classics of Christian devotion, Law's *A Serious Call*, available to ordinary readers. For an entire year they spent their time together in shortening the famous volume, chapter by chapter, without substantial harm to the content. When they completed the work, they were successful in getting Westminster Press to publish their edition, which has been widely distributed. Now, after more than twenty years of continuous existence, with inevitable changes in membership, the Yokefellow Group of the First Presbyterian Church, Fort Wayne, continues, and is actually stronger than ever before.

Several of those who assisted in the early articulation of the Yokefellow idea are no longer living, but their influence endures. Among them, in addition to Edward Gallahue, are Edwin Howe, a brilliant lawyer of Cleveland, and Wyatt Miller, a paint manufacturer of Chicago. The pattern of life of each person in the remarkable formative group was essentially similar. Nearly all had experienced periods of profound doubt, and nearly all had come into their Christian commitment in middle life, after long and agonized searching. All believed in the Church, imperfect as it is, but all realized that the Church needs within it new movements devoted consciously to renewal. All undertook to provide support both spiritual and financial to the implementation of their shared dream, realizing the joy of being involved in a new beginning. Though not one of them earned his living by being professionally religious, each one saw his daily work as an opportunity to engage in the ministry. One of their chief ministries was their willingness to become members of the Yoke-fellow board.

The board, seeing from the first the serious danger of overorganization, resolved consciously never to become administratively top-heavy. One consequence is that at the time of this writing, and in spite of inflation, the annual budget of Yokefellows International is only slightly higher than it was ten years earlier. The secret lies in being extremely careful with other people's money, and in using volunteer labor whenever it is available. The order of which we dreamed really exists, but not primarily as an organization. It is instead a redemptive movement markedly influenced by the principle of nonpossessiveness, with no copyrights on publications. Deliberate modesty appears even in the physical assets of the board, the international headquarters being located in a converted garage. Along with the nonpossessiveness has gone the rejection of a single stereotype. Thus the emphasis of Yokefellows on the West Coast has differed somewhat from the emphasis in other parts of the country. Instead of developing an educational center it seeks primarily to nourish small groups. The guiding spirit is Dr. Cecil Osborne.

One of those to whom contemporary Yokefellows owe much is the late Harold Duling, the first director of the Lilly Endowment, who attended the original lay conferences at Earlham College. Since it had not occurred to me to seek foundation assistance, Mr. Duling's approach was as surprising as it was encouraging. He knew that because of my responsibilities in 1954 and 1955, with the United States Information Agency, the Yokefellow work was temporarily in some abeyance. When he learned that I expected to return to full college duties in 1956, he felt that the time had come to lay greater stress on the Yokefellow idea. Accordingly, he wrote to me late in 1955, suggesting the possibility of the Lilly Endowment's providing matching funds. We accepted the offer with gratitude and had no difficulty in raising funds of our own to match the grant dollar for dollar. The simple method employed was that of recruiting persons termed Yokefellow Associates, each of whom was asked to represent the movement in his own area and to contribute a minimum of $100 a year. The plan worked so well that soon there was no need for a matching grant. In short, the original gift was looked upon as "seed money," with the hope that it would be required, so far as annual expenses are concerned, only in the germinal period. The interest which Lilly Endowment showed may now be seen in retrospect as the most important single lift which the Order of the Yoke has received. Mr. Duling's initial enthusiasm has been shared subsequently by his successor, John Lynn, and by Charles Williams, vice president for religion of the Lilly Endowment.

The first significant gathering which occurred when we determined, under the encouragement of the Lilly Endowment, to enlarge our work was attended by only three persons. Knowing how every meeting with Robert Greenleaf tended to produce new ideas and consequently new action, President Thomas E. Jones, of Earlham, and I went to Short Hills, New Jersey, for a day's conversation at the Greenleaf home. We had no prepared agenda and simply listened to one another as we sat on the porch in fine weather. Though we could not know what would come of such a meeting of minds, we were confident that something would emerge. What developed, largely because of Robert Greanleaf's imagination, were two new operating units, the Yokefellow Institute and the Earlham Institute for Executive Growth. Neither of these would probably ever have come into existence apart from the dialogue at Short Hills.

Mr. Greenleaf's contention that summer day was that new situations require new institutional developments. The parish congregation, valuable as it has been in the Christian Cause, frequently does almost nothing to implement the idea of the priesthood of every believer. The pastor is expected to do the work, while the contribution of the members is deemed satisfactory, even when it includes no more than occasional listening to sermons and the depositing of a little money in the offering. Participation is often limited to such a marginal operation as that of ushering! New vitality, we agreed, will not come until there is a radical change in expectations.

Mr. Greenleaf's vision of what is needed bears some resemblance to the monastic dream of the Middle Ages. Just as the monasteries were once centers of renewal, affecting entire areas of Christendom, so in our time there must be institutions for the training of men and women who can be involved in the ministry of common life. Because an untrained ministry is potentially harmful and may, in spite of noble motives, actually cause damage, there must be established a chain of educational centers geared to the contemporary need. Those centers should not, Mr. Greenleaf explained, be identical with theological seminaries, which exist to train the professionally religious, nor with centers devoted to social service, however valuable and necessary they are. We began to dream of an institute intrinsically different from any in existence, though a start had actually been made at Quaker Hill, north of Richmond, Indiana, where, beginning in 1947, I had led the first retreats of my career.

The first Yokefellow Institute was established in the house which my wife and I had owned, but which later belonged to Earlham. The house, where ten could sleep, seemed adequate in the beginning, but larger quarters were soon required, and a commodious structure was erected on the Earlham land across the ravine to the south of the main college buildings. The remarkable effectiveness of the Institute in influencing the church life of a wide area is chiefly the result of the dedication of the first director, Samuel Emerick, who was appointed in 1957 and who served until January 1974. Also important, both in the house on College Avenue and in the new structure, is the devotion of Leona Boyd, who has transformed cooking into a ministry.

In the new institute quarters there are sleeping rooms for thirty-six persons, dining facilities, bookstore, offices, library, lounge, and worship room. It is essentially a monastic establishment without any separation from the world and without any permanent residents. The usual retreat occupies forty-four hours, from six o'clock on Friday evening to two o'clock on Sunday afternoon. While various gatherings are planned during weekdays, the most productive time has proved to be the weekends because the aim is to reach the busy, employed people.

Since the establishment of the original Yokefellow Institute four others, serving a similar purpose, have come into existence. The first of these is the Tri-State Yokefellow Center, located in farming country twelve miles northwest of Defiance, Ohio, on the south edge of the village of Evansport. The Tri-State Institute occupies a converted bank barn, which has three levels, and sleeping accommodations for eighteen people. The most valuable part of the old building, the gift of Mr. and Mrs. Robert Pickering, was the oak frame. Attenders now are conscious of this solid structure because the beams are exposed in the rooms into which the barn is now divided. The building, being itself a symbol of conversion, is the scene in which, beginning in 1960, a great deal of new life has appeared. An adjunct is Hope House, devoted chiefly to private retreats on the part of individuals and couples who may feel the need to be away, not only from their daily work, but also from public meetings. The beneficent effect of Tri-State upon the churches in the surrounding towns is evident.

A more recent Yokefellow Center is Acorn, near Yorkville, Illinois, the building and surrounding woodland near the Fox River being the gift of the late Homer Dickson and his wife, Alice. James Shaver has from the first been the pioneer Yokefellow of Illinois. The Kentucky Yokefellow Center occupies some of the old buildings which once belonged to the Shaker Community thirty miles south of Lexington. There the sense of a noble past, combined with the determination to establish something more than a museum or a shrine, has helped to make Shaker Village into a remarkable instrument of renewal. The director, Stephen Sebert, who was especially trained for this particular opportunity, is influential in the spiritual life of a wide area in the Blue Grass section. The story of the growth and eventual decline of the Shaker community, sorrowful as it is, is a valuable spiritual asset. A still more recent development is that in North Carolina, guided by Jerry Murray.

When I began to think of a new kind of Christian fellowship I could not see very far down the road. That is why the innovative educational establishments came relatively late in the Yoke development. Another feature which we all value now, but which we did not see in the beginning, is the Annual Yokefellow Conference. After we had experienced one or two conferences, we realized that we were involved in a practice worthy of perpetuation. Thus each year since 1951 there has been held at Earlham College a general conference during spring vacation, when, because the students are away at that time, the residences can be occupied by conference attenders. I now see clearly that the long-established Christian practice of emphasizing a yearly gathering is eminently sound. Separated local groups, like separated individuals, need the encouragement which meeting others of like conviction can provide and which, it seems, can be provided in no other fashion. The Annual Yokefellow Conference, far from declining with the succeeding years as some movements do, grows steadily stronger. At the 1973 Conference more than two hundred persons had to be turned away from the opening dinner for lack of space, even though more people were crammed into the large Earlham dining room than had ever assembled there previously. One attraction was the address of Keith Miller, whom many of the Yokefellows across the nation had reason to know and to love. The Annual Conference is deliberately brief, running from six o'clock on a Friday evening to four o'clock Saturday afternoon.

Another feature of the growing fellowship, which I did not

envisage in advance, is that of the *Quarterly Yokefellow Letter.* Largely in response to requests of those on the mailing list, I now write, four times a year, a letter-essay of about fifteen hundred words devoted, not to promotion, but to ideas. What I find is that many dedicated Christians, being sincerely puzzled about a variety of theological questions, seek help in the clarification of their thinking. With that in mind, I have in the recent past written quarterly essays on "The Second Coming," "The Jesus People," "Speaking in Tongues," "Astrology," "The Decline of the Church," and other such topics of current interest. Since I have ceased to write a monthly column for *Quaker Life,* after doing so for eleven and a half years, the *Quarterly Yokefellow Letter* is now the only periodical writing in which I am engaged. It is possible for any person to become a regular recipient of the *Letter* simply by request, and without any financial consideration. Furthermore, any reader is free to copy and use the *Quarterly Yokefellow Letter* at his or her own discretion.

In my earlier years I gave very little thought to my fellow citizens who were imprisoned. Most of those whom I know were like me in that regard, chiefly because we had few reminders. Today all of that is changed, Yokefellows being especially conscious of those behind prison walls. The change began to come in my life during the summer of 1955, when I was asked to address a conference of prison chaplains meeting in the old Supreme Court room of the Capitol in Washington. I spoke on the power of the small group of people who have a common discipline and who share both their problems and their faith with one another. Though it had never occurred to me that such groups could be nurtured in prison communities, two of the chaplains present saw the possibilities and soon, working independently of each other, established Yokefellow Groups in the federal penitentiaries both at McNeil Island, near Tacoma, Washington, and at Lewisburg, Pennsylvania. So effective were these pioneer undertakings that the idea has spread until there are now more than five hundred such fellowships in various kinds of prisons across the country. The nurture of these is the responsibility of the Yokefellow Prison Ministry of which Newman Gaugler is president.

One result of the new development was that I began for the first time in my life to visit prisons and to make a few addresses to the prisoners. When I could, I took with me numerous Yokefellows from the outside. One highly amusing consequence of such speaking is that I now have in my study an autographed photograph of Abraham Lincoln, the signature looking startlingly authentic. The words are: "To Elton Trueblood with warm regards, A. Lincoln." The forgery is the work of a genuine professional who is serving a twenty-year sentence and who wished to share with me the only gift which he has at his disposal.

At the present time the vitality of the new order is still increasing. Lilly Endowment has generously provided challenge gifts for the creation of new educational centers, most of which become self-supporting after the initial assistance. Among the newest developments are those in England, in East Asia, including Japan, and in Switzerland. There are good prospects for new developments in both India and East Africa, the strategy being to train the leaders in America and then to provide them with support in their own lands.

During the last few years I have led many retreats, most of which have had five sessions of two hours each. The retreats I now value most are those which are entirely unprogrammed. It is my responsibility to guide each session in order to avoid, if possible, unprofitable discussions, but we have a complete absence of agenda, prepared speeches, reports, and minutes. We are able thereby to demonstrate a break with the standard practice of church gatherings, which are nearly always overprogrammed. The human results of this unconventional kind of meeting of minds are phenomenal.

The best of the unprogrammed retreats which I have led in recent years have been held at Lake Paupac Lodge, in Pennsylvania, and at Shakertown, Kentucky. All attenders are present by invitation and there is no publicity. Such gatherings were at first limited to younger men, but subsequently it has seemed wiser to invite couples so that the wives of the men can be involved in the thinking of their husbands. The couples are chosen solely on the basis of their promise as Christian leaders. One valuable by-product is that the attenders continue the fellowship begun in the forty-four-hour period and do help one another in a variety of ways. Without a program to inhibit participation, each person can share what means most to him or to her. With the right selection of attenders this is possible even with an attendance of fifty.

Much of my work as president of Yokefellows International has now developed into what I call the ministry of encouragement. Part of my inspiration for this is the striking admonition in what may be the earliest book of the New Testament, "Therefore encourage one another and build one another up, just as you are doing" (I Thessalonians 5:11). What I do chiefly in this direction is to try to help potential writers. Many, I find, need only slight assistance in order to be able to advance in their ability to communicate ideas. Lilly Endowment provides modest financial resources designed to liberate potential writers from the necessity of paid employment, so that for short periods they can develop their ideas single-mindedly. Several books, the product of such assistance, have now been published.

The future of the Yoke we cannot know, but we are at least convinced that certain features are of enduring value. If they decline in one pattern, they will need to arise in some other. The essentials are *commitment, discipline, ministry,* and *fellowship.* Without the *commitment* nothing else of any importance will occur; unless there is *discipline,* life dissolves in permissiveness; the *ministry* is too important to be limited to a professional class;

fellowship is essential because no person is strong enough to operate alone. The heart of the idea which has helped to give meaning to my own life for a quarter century is that, to be a Christian, *I must be yoked with others because I am yoked with Christ.*

Modest as our new order is, this one or something like it is what our time sorely needs, for it provides an alternative both to solitariness and to the impersonalism of the crowd. Since I first read the words of Archbishop Temple which serve as the epigraph of this chapter, I have been convinced that in the Christian Movement there will always be new and unexpected developments generation after generation. Just when the bones seem hopelessly dried, life arises. When I become discouraged, as sometimes I do, I remember the surprising creation of the Third Order of St. Francis seven hundred and fifty years ago. In like manner I think of the way in which the mood on both sides of the Atlantic was revolutionized by the Wesleys in the middle of the eighteenth century.

Each new development has been strictly unpredictable. Who could have predicted the work of Robert Raikes, in starting Sunday schools in 1780; or of George Williams, in dreaming up the Young Men's Christian Association in 1844; or of General William Booth, in establishing the Salvation Army in 1878? With such undoubted examples of inner renewal in mind, I expect others of equal significance in my lifetime, though I cannot possibly guess now what their precise character will be.

The Yokefellow Movement is best understood as part of the Renewal Movement of the twentieth century. Far from operating alone, it is closely affiliated with numerous other new forms of Christian fellowship. Going beyond the development envisaged by Francis, these together constitute a kind of "Fourth Order." Transcending the distinction between Protestant and Catholic, and including both pastors and ordinary members, they establish centers, bearing various names, which are necessary for the continuing reformation within the churches.

Twenty-five years ago I wrote in my journal that we need a contemporary counterpart of the Salvation Army. What I then envisioned was a fellowship that would do for the average thoughtful person what the Salvation Army has done for the poor and the dispossessed. I saw that even the people who denounce the Church do not denounce the Salvation Army because its devotion is obviously genuine. The Army has provided countless modest persons with a faith, a discipline, and a means of witness. I hope to live long enough to rejoice in new developments as effective as the one which Booth created nearly a century ago. It will not surprise me if the last quarter of the century with which my life has so far been contemporary becomes one of the most productive of all history, so far as the Christian faith is concerned. One of the most encouraging ideas which has entered my mind is that we are *early Christians*, still alive while the faith is fluid and capable of assuming new forms. I think that this idea was originated by Professor Kenneth Scott Latourette, but the origin is not really important. The important fact is that it is true.

7. *Father*

I have not the slightest doubt that domestic happiness is the greatest of all good gifts; next to that of "Wisdom" for which Solomon prayed.

Dean Inge

My family life has not, like my teaching and writing, been a separate vocation, but has been deeply involved in nearly all that I have tried to do. Observing the degree to which some public men lose their own children while they are working for good causes in the world, I determined to avoid that peril if I possibly could. We understood very early that family life is not automatic and that in it, as in so much else of human life, achievement does not come without effort and thoughtful planning. We found that is true in the use of time. Family affairs could not, we concluded, be assigned to the left-over space in the calendar, but must be scheduled with high priority. That is why even now I put birthday celebrations into the time schedule, getting them in before something else has preempted those precious hours.

Though Samuel Johnson had no children of his own, he understood how important the family tie is and was praying for his wife on the anniversary of her death, thirty years after the event. "The most authentic witnesses of any man's character," wrote the Rambler, "are those who know him in his own family." I believe this! If I do not gain and hold the love and respect of those who are nearest to me, outside reputation is of little value. Family life, of course, is strikingly unequal and we know that there are families which are scarred by deep hatreds, though this is something I could not bear.

Pauline Goodenow and I were married in a Quaker wedding in Rhode Island on August 24, 1924. Pauline had been my fellow student at Penn College, after which she taught school in Iowa for three years in an effort to repay the money she had borrowed for her education. Her Marshall ancestors, like my own, had moved from Indiana to Iowa in pioneer days. Though Pauline and I never met until we were in college together, we were aware that her grandparents and my grandparents had been acquainted with each other. Her grandfather, like my grandmother, was a recognized minister. We were the same kind of people, and our future looked bright.

With a small salary and a furnished house in Boston we believed that we could manage financially, while I studied at Harvard, without any paid employment on Pauline's part. After three demanding years of teaching it was a relief to her to be free to read on her own and to participate in what was fundamentally a joint task in the Friends Meeting of Boston. Pauline quickly joined the society made up of wives of Harvard graduate students and enjoyed new friendships which endured. Though she heard him only once, the influence of Charles William Eliot on her was substantial.

Early in December 1924 Pauline became desperately ill and subsequently spent many weeks in the hospital with no assurance of recovery. It looked as though all of our bright hopes were due to be blasted. She was pregnant, and the doctors seriously predicted that either the unborn child or the young mother would have to be sacrificed. The terrible winter, however, wore on as every day I went both to my classes at Harvard and to the New England Hospital for Women and Children. In the spring, when Pauline was able to travel by train, her mother came from Iowa and took her home, where she stayed until time for our first child to be born. Martin was born in my father's house on the family farm, July 26, 1925, and as soon as it was safe to travel, the three of us went back to Boston.

After the birth of our first child Pauline's health improved, but it deteriorated sharply soon after our removal to North Carolina. With the advantage of hindsight I see now that the pace of living which seemed reasonable to me was really too much for my young bride, whose courage always tended to obscure her physical weakness. In Greensboro we secured the services of an excellent physician who diagnosed Pauline's illness as pernicious anemia. By eating nearly raw liver and by using liver extract, she recovered rapidly in 1928 and soon was the strongest that she had been up to that time. Her second pregnancy, accordingly, was without difficulty and our son, Arnold, born January 2, 1930, was remarkably healthy from the beginning.

In our three years at Baltimore, and the following three years at Haverford, we were very proud of our two little boys and spent as much time with them as our duties would allow. The summer of 1934, spent on a farm near West Grove, Pennsylvania, provided a special opportunity to build family solidarity. The boys roamed the countryside with their dog, Socrates, and Martin learned to swim in the nearby creek. I was glad that for a while they could have an unhurried father.

Having two sons seemed to me fortunate, especially in the light of the repeated sickness of their mother, but after we were well settled at Stanford University, Pauline became so much stronger that she wished to have two more children. Responding as she did to the California climate and the happy life on the Stanford campus, Pauline experienced a great new burst of energy in 1938. On December 4, 1938, our third son, Samuel, was born, followed by our daughter, Elizabeth, on April 30, 1941.

Martin was almost sixteen and Arnold was eleven and a half when their sister arrived. The difference in age does not seem great now, but it seemed so then, the older boys taking much responsibility in the care of their little brother and sister.

Soon after the birth of Samuel I took Martin with me and traveled to England, an arrangement having been made for Pauline and the baby, with the help of a nurse, to spend the winter at Carmel. Arnold stayed with the Blake Wilburs so as to continue his schooling in Palo Alto. I had saved up my free academic quarters in order to have the winter and spring to spend as Fellow of Woodbrooke, at Birmingham, England, where I put Martin in an excellent local school for boys. In the evenings he joined me in the Woodbrooke Library and, though only thirteen, came to appreciate the style of the seventeenth-century writers in whose work I was then immersed. An amusing consequence was his choice of title for the diary he was keeping, "The Life and Gospel Labours of that Ancient Servant of Christ, Martin Trueblood." In the spring, when Sam was old enough to be left at Carmel with the nurse, Pauline joined us in Britain for the entire quarter. She enjoyed her first British experience, especially that in Edinburgh.

Soon after Elizabeth was born in 1941, I had the idea of taking Martin and Arnold on a pack trip on part of the Tahoe-Yosemite Trail, and it was one of the best things that we ever did. We took turns leading the pack horse, finding the trail increasingly difficult to follow as we went southward in very high country. Though we faced some genuine danger in an encounter with large bears, and though we felt cut off from civilized life, the experience drew the three of us together in a fashion which we have never forgotten. Because there were no others with us, there was nothing to divert our attention from our enjoyment of one another. I like to remember the days on the trail because, for a while, I was able to concentrate on the vocation of being a father. Teaching and writing played no part in our lives while the three of us walked, talked, slept, and ate in the High Sierras.

During the last years of the war the family group was separated because Martin was in the navy and Arnold was a student at Westtown School in Pennsylvania. Before going to Westtown Arnold had worked all summer, scrubbing floors in the coffee shop at Stanford, and had saved some money. As a trick he turned his savings into silver dollars, carrying one hundred of these in a canvas bag and surprising Easterners. With both older boys away our family was reduced to the two younger ones, to whom we gave all of our available attention. We built a picket fence around part of the garden so that Sam and his little sister could play there without wandering.

Inside the picket fence was a small cabin which had come to be something of a symbol of our life together. During our second summer at Stanford we had offered Martin and Arnold, then aged twelve and seven, a choice of expenditure on their behalf. We told them that we had set aside a sum sufficient to send both of them to camp or to purchase the materials for a cabin with bunk beds, which they could build among the redwoods on our place. With no hesitation they chose to build the cabin, and the experience was in every way a rewarding one. Cement and sand were delivered for the footings, and redwood boards, shingles, windows, and door for the structure itself. I gave some assistance on the footings, but after that the boys did it all with the exception of the work done by neighbor boys, who would gladly have paid for the privilege. The experience had enduring consequences, including the important one that Arnold later became a professional builder.

When we moved to Stanford, we were determined to have our own home largely because we thought ownership is good for children. The task was not easy to accomplish, however, because I was still in debt for my graduate study, but we were able to secure sufficient loans. The building of the play cabin was one of many dividends which came from ownership, however tenuous it was. Our children could have privileges on our own place which would not have been possible had we lived in rented property. The same motivation influenced our decision, after our removal to Richmond, to purchase the old house on College Avenue. It was almost too large to be cared for easily, but the children loved it, and beginning in December 1950 we had the blessed assistance of Leona Boyd. Help was necessary because even then, Pauline's strength was beginning to fail. This will explain the dedication of our joint book, *The Recovery of Family Life,* published in 1953. The dedication is: "To Martin and Arnold and Samuel and Elizabeth, who came into our home involuntarily, to Margaret and Caroline, who came by choice, and to Leona Boyd, able cook and housekeeper, who set one of us free to write." Margaret and Caroline were, at that time, our only daughters-in-law.

Both at Stanford and in the early days at Earlham we faced serious problems with Sam's asthma. Upon medical advice we tried to protect him from dust, even going so far as to construct a dust-proof room in the College Avenue house. What really succeeded, however, was a temporary change in climate. When I was writing *The Common Ventures of Life* in the hill country of Texas, we had the younger children with us. Since Sam was nine and Elizabeth was six and a half, both were enrolled in Richmond schools, but the authorities agreed that the Texas experience would counterbalance the lack of school attendance, especially if Pauline guided their studies, as she did. We loved our life together in the Heart-of-the-Hills Inn, the children riding ponies in their free time and Sam becoming stronger every day. The freedom from the northern winter developed his health to a point that no serious problem of allergies has ever returned. Nine years later he became a varsity football player.

Partly with the education of our younger children in mind, we drove slowly through the Deep South in March 1948 en route from Texas to Virginia. The big ante-bellum houses of Natchez,

Mississippi, were open for visitors, and we took advantage of the opportunity thus afforded. All of us appreciated the great houses, but Pauline appreciated them most of all. Our immediate destination was Lexington, Virginia, where I was to be awarded by Washington and Lee University my first honorary degree, Doctor of Letters. I value it because I gave nothing to get it, not even a commencement address. Furthermore, we are not likely to hear a voice as golden as that of President Francis P. Gaines. He represented the quintessence of the eloquent speech of the Old South.

As fully as we could, we developed our stop at Washington and Lee into a family project. Sam and Elizabeth, young as they were, could sit in the auditorium and hear the citation which Francis P. Gaines delivered with such grace. We enjoyed lunch in the very house which General and Mrs. Lee occupied in the last period of their lives. The children felt that they were participating in their father's career. Unfortunately, many children are given too little opportunity to know at first hand about the lives of their parents.

Upon our return home from Texas and Virginia we faced a serious problem. Arnold, then a senior in Richmond High School, had contracted a terrible kind of pneumonia which for many weeks failed to respond to any known medication. Even after we transferred him from the Richmond hospital to Christ Hospital, Cincinnati, with eminent lung specialists in charge, he became steadily worse and we had to face the possibility of losing him. In the midst of the crisis I received a telephone call from New York, offering hope. On the telephone was William B. Bell, then president of the American Cyanamid Company, who, having learned of Arnold's severe illness, told me of a new medicine which as yet had no name but in which he had reason to believe. Being desperate, I told him to send it by air mail. I took it to the specialist at Christ Hospital, who had never heard of it, but who, because he also was desperate, decided to try it. In a few days our son's temperature returned to normal and within a week he was home. The medicine was eventually named *aureomycin*.

One important part of our family life at Earlham was the care of our big vegetable garden. In the garden, located on the edge of the campus where our house is now, we grew as much of our food as we could, rejoicing in its freshness. Believing in work, we expected the children to help with the weeding, but I encountered one objection which I could not answer. One summer Sam, when he was about eight years old, said, "Dad, just because gardening is your hobby, is that any reason why it should be mine?" I did not know what to say then, and I do not know now.

A major family project, especially in 1952, was the restoration of the house in which we then lived and which had stood for nearly a century. We had the problem of living in it while parts of the building were radically altered, but we were able to do so without intolerable strain. Part of our task, paradoxically, was to undo some of the "modernization" performed fifty years earlier. It was a special joy to eliminate the gas fire in the living room fireplace, to prepare again for the burning of logs, and to install an old mantel to restore the original appearance, in so far as that was possible. Pleasurable also was the leveling of floors that with the years had become uneven. We covered the worst of them with cork tiles. In the end we had an Early American home of which we could be proud, our pride being shared by our children.

One of the best aspects of our family life during those years was the setting aside of a regular family night. We knew how harmful it is to children when they are forced to compete at all times with public events for the attention of their parents. Sometimes we observed that the children of public-spirited parents may actually suffer more than do those not so involved. The idea occurred to us that we could have one evening each week

when there would be no competition at all, and when consequently our children could feel that they had our undivided
attention.

We chose Mondays for the family emphasis, and the plan was
a success. We tried to get the word around. Other people, we
said, were free to have committee meetings on Monday evenings
if that was their desire, but we wanted them to know that we
would not be present. We could then do a variety of things at
home or attend motion pictures if that was what the children
desired. Sometimes, munching abundant popcorn, we sat by the
fire and told stories; sometimes we played games; sometimes we
just talked and laughed and made plans for the future.

As I look back now, I see that even though there were always
problems, our family life at the period just described was very
good. Martin elected to take a senior year at Earlham, in order
to have more liberal arts, after the completion of his engineering
training at Notre Dame and his experience as a naval officer on
the sea. His year with us before his marriage in June 1947
brought him close again to his younger brothers and sister.
Across that beautiful picture of family life there came, however,
the increasing shadow of Pauline's illness, which became really
serious in 1954. In the spring of that year we had our last big
house party, with Martin and his family home from his second
naval duty. Pauline was able to enjoy her four children, two
daughters-in-law, and four grandchildren in a really happy gathering, extending over several days of spring vacation. Within six
months she was paralyzed and on February 7, 1955, she died,
aged fifty-three, after being my wife a little more than thirty
years.

Subsequent to Pauline's death in the Washington area we
held a memorial service for her in the Earlham College meetinghouse. The service was a triumphal occasion, ending, as all stood,
with the singing by the concert choir of Handel's Hallelujah
Chorus. Many people spoke spontaneously of her life and faith,

one of the most moving messages being that of President Thomas E. Jones.

As I recall those difficult months, I am deeply grateful that Pauline, weak as she was in her last year, was able to participate in two public experiences which gave her a sense of fulfillment. The first was her address at New Haven before the National Assembly of the Congregational Churches, and the second was her attendance at Evanston, in August 1954, as a delegate to the Assembly of the World Council of Churches. At Evanston it was her peculiar satisfaction to give a tea for the wife of the Archbishop of Canterbury, a lady whose acquaintance she much valued. Already, the brain tumor must have been growing, but we did not of course know about it then.

When the Evanston gathering was over, Pauline went to Pen Point, the Pocono Mountain retreat which we had been developing, and she was able to stay there ten days after the house was completed. She was there alone, except for our daughter, Elizabeth, and it was one of the happiest experiences of her life, though her strength was inadequate for any day. Because she loved Pen Point above all places, it was good that she could enjoy it for even a little while in its finished state.

Pen Point is one private home in the new community called Lake Paupac, located on the edge of the wilderness sixteen miles north of Buck Hill Falls. The post office is Greentown, and the nearest place for shopping is Newfoundland. Lake Paupac is a natural lake one mile long and a half mile wide, fed principally by the stream from Promised Land, and emptying to the southwest in a deep gorge with two waterfalls. At present the community, largely of summer people, is housed in more than forty cottages, with dining facilities and guest quarters located in Lake Paupac Lodge. The cottages are clustered inconspicuously about the lake, with more than a thousand acres of unspoiled woodland behind them. Although the area has been sparsely occupied for a long time, the present operation did not begin until 1950.

We had been dreaming of a summer place for several years, but had no idea where we might find it. We had in mind something which might become an encouragement to family solidarity, and since our children appeared to be settling in Pennsylvania, a summer home in that state seemed reasonable. We knew that families often scatter so much that the children of the brothers and sisters hardly know one another, and only by deliberate effort could we avoid that from happening to us.

Just when we were about ready to consider a place seriously, I accepted the invitation to deliver an address on the two hundred fiftieth anniversary of the founding of Gwynedd Meeting in Montgomery County. Roger Hallowell met our train at Paoli and soon began telling of the exciting new community which he and some other Swarthmoreans were planning in the wilderness area of the Pocono Mountains. Because that sounded like an answer to our search, Pauline stayed over, when I had to return to my teaching, and drove with Mrs. Hallowell to spy out the land. Since I had told her that I would support her judgment, she chose a lot at once. The lot was one with considerable elevation, the unique feature being a high stone ledge which she envisioned as one wall of an outdoor living room. Her ashes now lie embedded in this natural wall.

Officially we became part of the pioneer group at Paupac even though we waited four years to build our dwelling house. Meantime, we constructed my writing cabin, in which we camped for a while as we developed the rough terrain. The many miles of wilderness to the east of the cabin are inhabited by only an abundance of wild life. Often, as I have looked up from my writing, I have enjoyed seeing the deer just outside the window.

During the first summer of operation my wife and younger children went with me to England where I was needed as chairman of the Friends World Committee, but Arnold, then aged twenty, remained at Paupac and drove the truck for the corporation. On his weekly days off he erected the frame, roof, and walls of the study, which was accordingly ready for completion in the summer of 1951. At that time I did part of the work myself, adding the floor and porches and helping with the fireplace. The physical work was a beneficent change for me, but it meant that I wrote no book that summer.

After the cabin was completed, four of us sometimes slept in it, and while we were a little crowded, we did not mind. The cabin has two high bunks on opposite sides of the fireplace chimney, and into these Sam and Elizabeth were able to fit perfectly. Meanwhile, we cleared the ground for the cottage and spent many hours in planning how it would be arranged. Pauline and Arnold did the major designing and drew the plans. We were able to employ a skilled local craftsman to manage the actual construction, and we have been happy with the result. By the summer of 1954, when the actual work was done, Sam, aged fifteen, was large enough to serve as the mason's helper, carrying the heavy stones which went into the chimney. All of us felt that in one way or another we were participants in a family enterprise. The enduring stone masonry at both ends of the outdoor living room was all done by Arnold, who by that time was both carpenter and mason. One project which our children enjoyed was that of finding a stone shaped like the end of a fountain pen, lettering it, and placing it at the entrance to the driveway. Everyone seems to understand how the name originated. Actually, the greater part of nine books have been written at Pen Point.

In the years since the death of their mother my children have valued Pen Point even more, because they know how deeply she loved it, and how she hoped that it would hold them together. Consequently, they have not limited their visits to the summer months, but have used the retreat at various seasons. Some enjoy the winter, with the excellent skating, as much as the summer beauty.

The Paupac community soon became one marked by mutual

affection, summer ties tending to become unusually close. This has carried over to the second generation who have organized what they call a Society of Freeloaders. The friendships in this group are nurtured throughout the year, but they never would have been started apart from the beautiful summer days together, with the swimming, boating, and hiking.

After enjoying Pen Point for twenty years, I felt increasingly that it was time for me to turn it over to my children. Since it was soon obvious that it could not be managed efficiently by so many, my eldest son, Martin, is now the owner and corporation member. There is thus a strong probability that a prized bit of earth will be in the possession of my descendants for several generations.

On August 5, 1956, I married Virginia, the widow of Marion Zuttermeister and the mother of Henry and Virginia, both minors at the time. As the daughter of Simeon Hodgin, formerly city engineer of Richmond, Indiana, and his wife, Estelle Godard, she stems from a North Carolina Quaker ancestry similar to my own. A graduate of Miami University, Oxford, Ohio, Virginia has many intellectual and cultural interests. After the death of her first husband she was employed in various capacities at Earlham College, while living in Richmond with her children. At the time of our marriage, which took place in the Washington Cathedral, she was assistant to Dr. Ronald Bridges of the United States Information Agency in Washington. By marrying Virginia I enlarged my family in that, between us, we now have six children and fourteen grandchildren.

A frequent inquiry in conversation is whether any one of my three sons follows in my footsteps. The answer is negative, if the question concerns a specific career, but affirmative, if general interests are meant. Martin, after his second period of naval service, was employed for sixteen years by the Standard Pressed Steel Company of Jenkintown, Pennsylvania. In 1970 he made a radical shift in his career, giving up his work as an engineer and accepting a position as administrator of Foulke Ways, the Friends retirement home at Gwynedd, Pennsylvania. Martin finds that he enjoys his work with elderly people, many of whom clearly look upon him as a kind of extra son.

Arnold has been a builder and developer of land in Montgomery County, Pennsylvania, for eighteen years. The new Village Center at Spring House and the neighboring Toll House Square are tangible evidences of his imagination. Increasingly, he gives time to public service in his community, including that of Gwynedd Friends Meeting.

Samuel, my third son, now admitted to the bar in New York and Pennsylvania, as well as Indiana, is president of Penn-Eastern Development Company with offices at Spring House. After graduation from Duke University Law School Sam practiced with a firm in Indianapolis and then taught law for a year at the University of Khartoum in the Sudan. On his return to America, and before entering land development with his brother, he practiced in New York with a Broadway firm. He and his wife, Betsy, now live near Ambler, Pennsylvania.

Elizabeth, my daughter, is married to Daniel Derr, who is employed in the Federal Land Bank located at Bel Air, Maryland. The Derrs, who have three small children, live on a farm about a mile from the Susquehanna River, in Cecil County, which provides the scene for a good way of life. Elizabeth is an active member of the Deer Creek Friends Meeting, a connection which I prize because my admiration for Deer Creek Friends was developed during my Baltimore days.

Henry Zuttermeister, Virginia's son, lives in Fort Wayne, Indiana, where he is employed as a social worker with a deep interest in adequate housing. His wife, Phyllis, is a librarian with the Fort Wayne Public Library. Virginia's daughter, Virginia, now Mrs. Arthur Grohs, lives in Susanville, California, where her husband is engaged in a mercantile career.

The fact that my three sons live in the same Pennsylvania

community means that when I see one, I can see all. Furthermore, their sister, in Maryland, is not far away. Henry, with his family, is close enough for frequent contact, and I encourage Virginia to visit the Grohs family in California at least once each year. Before the younger Virginia was married, mother and daughter toured Europe together. On the *Queen Elizabeth* coming home, one of the fellow passengers was Arthur Grohs of California, who was married to our daughter a year later. According to the story, he noticed the mother first, but I am not sure that this is true.

Because of Virginia's love of travel I was glad in the autumn of 1964 that we could go around the world together, taking advantage of the Doan teaching award. We went by freighter from San Francisco to Suez, completing our journey home by land and air travel. That was the first experience for both of us in either the Far East or the Middle East, and we loved all of it. I had with me, in addition to the Holy Bible, only two books, the *Complete Works of Shakespeare* and Gibbon's *Decline and Fall of the Roman Empire.* We like to remember our first visit to Japan and our only visit to Okinawa. Because Virginia took excellent photographs of every important scene, I did not even carry a camera. One interesting family connection in Greece was that in the Adrian Hotel, in the old part of Athens, we occupied the very same room which had been occupied previously by Virginia's brother and his wife. Best of all, the windows of this room face the Acropolis.

In our own country, recreational journeys have usually been combined with speaking engagements. Thus in January 1973 I decided to speak in Tampa and St. Petersburg, with unhurried days between engagements when we could enjoy the freedom from ice and snow. I was especially glad for Virginia to have restful days of this kind after she had driven our car from Indiana to Florida. As we sat on the beach of the Gulf of Mexico, I wrote a limerick which was apparently enjoyed:

My wife's a fabulous beauty,
And even in age she's a cutey;
She sits in the sun,
And thinks it is fun,
To be far, far away from her duty.

Somewhat later my wife, feeling that it was her responsibility to respond in kind, composed the following:

My husband's a college professor,
And sometimes a Father Confessor,
He writes with a pen
And's in bed by ten;
After putting his watch on the dresser.

Another pattern of expression which we share is that of the palindrome. It pleases us that the Zip Code number of our address, 47374, conforms to this interesting pattern. We try to come up with original forms, hoping to find one as good as "deified," but this is extremely difficult to match. When we travel together by car, my wife watches for palindromes on the speedometer and informs me when they are about to appear. I soon learned the trick of letting my wife do all of the driving when we travel by car together. This is not only because she is an excellent driver, but also because this division of labor sets me free to write down ideas as they occur to me, or to sleep if I am particularly tired. Furthermore, she can never, on this basis, criticize my driving.

Frequently, as we drive together or sit at home with none others present, my wife and I play a game in which our love of poetry is a necessary feature. One of us will say a line from some well-known poem and then we try to keep going as we take turns, repeating alternate lines. Happily, both of us, though as children we lived in different sections of the country, learned many poems that have become enduring resources. That is one of the reasons why neither of us is ever bored.

After our marriage Virginia and I put a good deal of thought into the right location of our residence. With the College Avenue house sold back to Earlham and slated to be used as the Yokefellow Institute, we decided to purchase a house on the east side of Richmond and thus to be identified with the city rather than merely with the college. We occupied the house for nearly ten years before we decided to build our own dream house on the edge of the Earlham campus. In preparation for building, after selling our city house, we occupied a college apartment which is a twin of that which was occupied by the former president, Thomas E. Jones. Living in the same building with Tom Jones and his second wife, Betty, whom he married after we had joined him, was a valuable experience. Betty was the widow of Paul Furnas, who, as comptroller, had been a member of the new team which came to Earlham in 1946. The odd new fact was that the three families, which had come to Earlham together, were all finally represented under one roof, each with a new partner. Now that both Tom and Betty are gone, I am the sole survivor of the original six. Betty and I had an extra bond in that we had five grandchildren in common, her daughter, Caroline, being the wife of my son, Arnold.

We knew the optimum location of our new retirement home, but there were many problems, largely because the land no longer belonged to us. The desired location was the former scene of my vegetable garden, side by side with Teague Library and facing the great sweep of lawn reminiscent of an English park.

In building our new house, we had no need to hurry. As early as the spring of 1967, while we were in London, Virginia corresponded with the same architect who had designed Teague Library a few years earlier. All agreed on the closest possible approximation to Williamsburg style, both externally and internally. My wife, who had already visited Williamsburg many times, admired the work of restoration. Accordingly, when our house was completed, we named it Virginia Cottage. Above the fireplace, behind the mantel, we left a record of the building, aware that sometime in the long future someone may read it. We included the names of both the architect and the builder, along with the Biblical quotation, "Prepare thy work without, and make it fit for thyself in the field; and afterwards build thine house" (Proverbs 24:27, AV).

The text from Proverbs seemed appropriate in that I had toiled long in the field and finally could have a place where I could remain if I desired to do so. There was space for the display of the reminders of our experiences in many parts of the world. Since I had a separate study next door, I did not need one in the new house, but I wanted Virginia to have one of her own, and that she now has. There she collects, sorts, and enjoys the many photographic slides of her travels.

We like being on the edge of the campus, yet with our own bird sanctuary, with numerous birds being visible from our breakfast table. We decided to have two stories, partly to keep our knees supple and partly to separate the sleeping quarters from the living quarters. Though most of my books and manuscripts are in Teague Library, I do have a nook in my bedroom, with an easy chair, a good light, and bookcases on both sides. To my left is the *Encyclopaedia Britannica* while to the right is the Yale University edition of the works of Dr. Samuel Johnson. Often, as we were planning to build, I thought of Willa Cather's novel *The Professor's House*. That is what ours is, and we love it. We occupied it in July 1971, and expect to live in it unto the last for either of us. After that, the house will belong unconditionally to Earlham College.

We are glad that we built *after* most of our life experiences rather than earlier. Only as one approaches the conclusion can he begin to understand the purpose of his life and what it is that he needs. Thus, the building of a house is comparable to the writing of a book, in which the preface is often composed last because it is only in fulfillment that purpose can become clear. Only after living many years can a man and a woman, in full partnership, know what it is that they need. "A thing," said Aristotle, "is more properly said to be what it is when it has attained to fulfillment than when it exists potentially." I learned from William Temple the great idea that the meaning of a poem often becomes clear only when the last line is reached. Thus the end illumines the whole! In any case I am convinced that people build better if they build in maturity.

8. Rambler

Even pleasing scenes improve by time, and seem more exquisite in recollection than when they were present.

James Boswell

In the final number of the *Idler*, one of the most appealing of all of the literary productions of Dr. Samuel Johnson, the wise man wrote, "There are few things, not purely evil, of which we can say, without some emotion of uneasiness: This is the last." Being now somewhat older than Johnson was when he wrote these unforgettable lines, I think I understand a little of what Johnson meant. In 1970 I taught my last class in any college, and I do not expect to conduct any more examinations. On July 6, 1973, I gave my last address at a pastors' school, finishing at what may be the best of them, that at Furman University, Greenville, South Carolina. After writing several hundred editorials and columns, I completed the last of this particular kind of journalism in June 1973.

In the light of these experiences I now reach the conclusion that lastness is not really so bad as Dr. Johnson reported. Though any particular finality is sobering, it need not be sad. Certainly it is not sad if each ending provides for new beginnings. It is in this spirit that I face the remaining years of my life, in which the conclusion of certain experiences merely opens the way to the enjoyment of others. Some of the new experiences may be far away and utterly different from anything which I have encountered before. I know that Epictetus warned, "If you are an old man, never even get far away from the ship, for fear that when He calls, you may be missing," but I do not intend to heed these particular words of the Stoic philosopher. I believe that I can answer His call whether I am at home or far away.

For a long time before my actual retirement in June 1966 I looked forward to it with keen anticipation, preparing for it as carefully as I could. Often I contemplated the wonder of retirement, providing it can be seen as liberation for new service, rather than a denial of further usefulness. It is a common experience these days for someone to approach me and say, "But you are not really retired." What am I to say in reply? The only reasonable answer, though a cruel one, is to point out that the remark reveals a curious misunderstanding of what retirement means. I suspect that what the person really thinks is that retirement means playing shuffleboard or even dominoes or watching television endlessly. The alternative to this foolishness is to see retirement as the opportunity for the freedman to engage in what he thinks he ought to do.

The decision to take retirement at sixty-five made possible what is undoubtedly the most enjoyable period of my life. I have been blessed with excellent health, never having been a hospital patient. Though in 1966 President Bolling offered me the option of annual extensions of my teaching, I declined. Like the fabulous Mark Hopkins, I retired because I did not want anyone to ask why I did not. It was my ultimate chance to apply my own doctrine that life is lived best when it is lived in chapters.

Since retirement my wife and I have been able to do what Horace advised:

> Sworn to no master's arbitrary sway,
> I range where're occasion points the way.

First we went to London and settled down for many months in what seems to us the world's most fascinating city. Though it has been nearly three hundred years since our ancestors left there, we feel a real bond with both the past and the present. After studying the life and thought of Robert Barclay for twenty-eight years, it was a keen pleasure to visit Ury, Barclay's old Scottish estate, and to enjoy there the gracious hospitality of Lord and Lady Stonehaven, who showed us the "Houff" where generations of Barclays are buried. We liked rambling about Gordonstoun, where Barclay was born, and where is now located the famous school attended earlier by Prince Philip, and at the time of our visit, by Prince Charles.

Traveling in Britain may give the American the exact combination of familiarity and strangeness which is so gratifying. "Men require of their neighbours," wrote Whitehead, "something sufficiently akin to be understood, something sufficiently different to provoke attention, and something great enough to command admiration." Though we went leisurely on around the world in an easterly direction, we found no place to surpass London in interest. In the heart of London I had many reminders of the man who has so deeply influenced my life, and who wrote the *Rambler,* the *Adventurer,* and the *Idler.*

The problem of what to call this last chapter of my autobiography has not been an easy one. I toyed with the idea of calling it Freedman or Elder or Gardener, but rejected all of these rather easily. The most appealing title, for a while, was Traveler, but this was not really accurate inasmuch as my travels are by no means constant. Finally, Johnson's term for himself, when he was the anonymous author of his most famous set of essays, seemed to provide the desired solution. I chose a term partly humorous, recognizing that even though the term sometimes indicates aimless wandering, this is not the connotation which I have in mind. What I want to suggest is a life of maximum freedom to achieve conscious purposes whether at home or abroad. I want to indicate both freedom to go, and freedom not to go.

The Rambler did not actually travel very much, preferring usually to remain in London. His tour of Scotland and the Hebrides, recounted in both his own *Journey* and Boswell's *Tour,* is memorable because it was unusual. In any case he called himself Rambler long before a visit to Scotland was even contemplated. The Doctor told Sir Joshua Reynolds how he had selected the name by which he was long known. "I was at a loss how to name it," he told Reynolds. "I sat at night upon my bedside, and resolved that I would not go to sleep till I had fixed its title. The *Rambler* seemed the best that occurred, and I took it." After producing two essays a week for two years, Johnson concluded the series, convinced that the traveler need not follow, endlessly, the same road. In the last of the essays he wrote, "Time, which puts an end to all human pleasures and sorrows, has likewise concluded the labours of the *Rambler."* After what had been drudgery, he was free at last.

However greatly we may value work, there is undoubted pleasure in its cessation. The author of a long book counts the pages, looking with anticipation to the writing of the final page. The sensitive reader can readily understand and appreciate the emotion of Edward Gibbon when he wrote the last line of the monumental work on which he had toiled for years. The public speaker, looking at his calendar, views with satisfaction the point in his schedule when there are no more engagements. Dr. Johnson was speaking for all who have too much to do when in the final *Rambler* he depicted with deathless prose the problem of the person who must produce work on schedule. "He that condemns himself to compose on a stated day," he wrote, "will often bring to his task an attention dissipated, a memory embarrassed, an imagination overwhelmed, a mind distracted with anxieties, a body languishing with disease: He will labour on a barren topick, till it is too late to change it; or in the ardour of invention, diffuse into wild exuberance, which the pressing hour of publication cannot suffer judgment to examine or reduce."

This famous paragraph is one of the factors in my decision to free myself from a whole chain of relentless promises. I may give more speeches, but I shall give them less frequently and without a sense of pressure or the demands of regularity. I have greatly admired Dr. Harry Emerson Fosdick's decision to end his speaking engagements at a fixed date. He had had, he decided, abundant opportunities and therefore needed no more. He did not wish to be remembered for productions which would reflect declining vitality or mere repetition of what had been said better at an earlier time. It was part of the wisdom of Dr. Johnson that in his numerous literary projects he knew how to end, as well as how to begin.

Though much of my time during my first year of freedom from academic duties was spent at Friends House Library in Barclay research and writing, I still had days when I could cultivate the friendship of living persons. As something of a revelation it suddenly occurred to me that if there was anyone whom I really wanted to meet, there was no good reason for not trying to do so. My first experiment in the adventure in friendship was the writing of a brief letter to the Bishop of Coventry. I told him that I had read *Fire at Coventry* and that I desired to meet the man who had lived at the center of a movement of renewal in connection with the dedication of the new cathedral. I had visited Coventry in 1946, when I became acquainted with the former bishop and listened to the first plans involving the erection of a totally new structure. Naturally, I wanted to see the results.

To my surprised delight I received, in a day or so, a note from Cuthbert Bardsley, the present Bishop of Coventry, inviting me to come to lunch at his episcopal residence and to bring Virginia with me. So well did we get along that day that Bishop Bardsley invited us back as his overnight houseguests. During that second experience of friendship with one who had so recently been a stranger, we discovered that our host is a splendid amateur painter, as well as a spiritual leader. When my wife admired one of his paintings more than others, he immediately presented it to her. The canvas now hangs in Virginia Cottage.

Our pleasant interlude at Coventry encouraged us to try again. I therefore wrote to Dr. J. B. Phillips, whose translation of the Greek New Testament I had employed for a long time. In my brief note, addressed to Dr. Phillips at his home about one hundred thirty miles south of London, I said simply that we should like to call on him and his wife. Promptly, the good man replied, inviting us to visit them, and that we did when we were in their area for another reason. Far from resenting the intrusion, the Phillips couple seemed to welcome our visit, which is one we can never forget. We saw then, better than we had seen before, how marvelous the Christian fellowship is. Though it is possible to live close to neighbors on the same street for years without knowing them at all, a truly Christian fellowship can be achieved in a short time. This is because the basis of fellowship is not geographical proximity, but something much more significant: a common commitment.

Later, during our long London stay, other new contacts brought similar results. The most agreeable were with the Dean of St. Paul's Cathedral, the Dean of Westminster Abbey, and the Archbishop of York. I concluded that prominent people are much more approachable than we normally suppose. In any case, they may be as eager for friendship as are the rest of us. Furthermore, I found that I could learn from new persons, trying usually to guide the conversation into the fields of the other man's greatest interest and competence. In this way conversation, ceasing to be casual, can become educational.

In Geneva the high point of our stay was not connected with any of the famous sights, but was a dinner with Dr. and Mrs. Paul Tournier. There was much to bring us together, since the doctor had spoken to the Annual Yokefellow Conference in Indiana, and we were associated with the same publisher. As I listened to Paul Tournier, I rejoiced in the degree to which his central idea of treating the whole person is catching on in the modern world. There is much experiential support for his conviction that psychiatry is more successful if it is not isolated from the rest of the healing process.

One of the verifications of my new insight about the availability of prominent men came in India. I was eager to see Dr. Radhakrishnan on his own ground, largely because he illustrates so well the Platonic pattern which combines political responsibility with the philosophical vocation. Accordingly, while we were in New Delhi, I addressed a note to the former president of India at his home in Madras, saying we wished to call on him. The approach was easy because in a former year he had spoken at Earlham. When we reached our Madras hotel, we found a note from Dr. Radhakrishnan, inviting us to tea at his house. We enjoyed greatly the subsequent conversation, in which we were able to deal frankly with serious issues, one of which was the Indian veneration of the cow.

After an unhurried stay in Japan we returned to America by way of Alaska in October 1967 and settled into a full life, not only of writing, but also of speaking in many parts of the nation. By that time, since the passenger service on the railroads had been sharply curtailed, nearly all of the travel had to be done by air. That was sorrowful to me because I had loved the trains almost with a passion. Indeed, one of our reasons for settling at Earlham College in 1946 was that Richmond, Indiana, was then an excellent railroad center. Pennsylvania Station was a busy and important place, with a good restaurant and trains going regularly in five directions. Each day there were famous trains, such as The Spirit of St. Louis and the Penn-Texas, carrying large numbers of passengers both east and west. It was an adventure to take one of the trains at Richmond in the early evening, dine aboard, and arrive well rested the next morning in New York, Philadelphia, or Washington. Because we sometimes sat up all night in order to save money, the common Quaker joke in Richmond was, "Are you going Pullman or Woolman?" To the initiated that referred to the experience of John Woolman who, on the sea, deliberately rode in the steerage in order to demonstrate his identification with the life of the poor.

As the trains declined, Dayton, Ohio, proudly advertising itself as the birthplace of aviation because of the Wright brothers, developed an excellent airport. Since the completion of the new Interstate Highway 70, Richmond residents can now reach the airport almost as easily as can the people of downtown Dayton. Thus our transportation problem is largely solved. Like any traveler, I soon discovered that there are many disappointments. I learned, however, that long hours of waiting, rightly used, could become among the most productive in my life.

Lewis Mumford, when he was my colleague at Stanford University, had introduced me earlier to the wisdom of carrying numbers of government postcards. An ordinary person, he taught me, can write a postcard in less time than it takes to make a telephone call, even though it is a local one. It became my invariable practice, in the days of almost constant travel, to carry enough cards to supply me in all contingencies. Sometimes I found that without much difficulty I could write as many as twenty cards in an hour. By posting them in whatever airport I happened to sit at the time, my little messages were on their way without delay. I was much less likely to send such messages if I had to hunt envelopes and stamps, whereas the use of the postcard is simplicity itself. A pleasant extension of the postcard habit, when a quick reply is essential, is that of enclosing with a letter a self-addressed postcard. I have done this especially when corresponding with my children.

The notion that time is no longer important to the retired person is not necessarily true. With advancing age time becomes increasingly precious, the recognition that it is limited heightening its value. For this reason I have long gone to bed at ten o'clock, and make it a general rule to be at my desk in Teague Library at seven o'clock each morning, especially when I am writing. The hour from seven to eight is, for me, the most productive one of the entire day, not only because I am stronger when fully rested, but also because of the almost total absence of interruptions. To use rightly the time we still have is a sacred obligation.

One of my best time savers is to have lunch in my library. I have installed a small refrigerator in which to keep milk and a few other items of perishable food. By having a simple sandwich and a glass of milk in my library I protect my wife from interruption in the middle of the day and save time for the rest that I need. After lunch I sleep on the sofa for a half hour and rise refreshed for the interviews and other duties which afternoons always bring.

A short but valued period of my retirement is that associated with Mt. Holyoke College, in which I was appointed Purington Lecturer for the winter and spring of 1970. I had long had connections with Mt. Holyoke as a visiting preacher, beginning in my Haverford days, but living at South Hadley for a semester as a member of the academic community was a radically different experience. One connection with the past, however, appeared when I was driven to the airport. My college driver was the same man who had first met me at the Springfield railroad station thirty-five years before. At least something was enduring! Our closest associates at Mt. Holyoke were Professor and Mrs. Robert Berkey, whose continuing friendship we prize. It was a special pleasure to visit them two years later in Cambridge, England.

While we were at Mt. Holyoke, the oldest of the women's colleges was toying with the idea of becoming coeducational, but President David B. Truman has successfully resisted the pressure for uniformity. The result is that Mt. Holyoke remains a college for women. This seems to me a wise decision, not because a women's college is necessarily a better one, though that is arguable, but because a women's college is one option which ought to be kept open as a possibility in our culture.

I found in 1970 that I enjoyed my teaching, and I was especially glad to round out my experience in this particular way. I now know at first hand what it is to teach in a college for men, in institutions for both sexes, and finally in a college for women. Every time I walked through Mary Lyon Gate, I felt a conscious appreciation of a really noble heritage. The high point of the semester was a service of worship in which we tried to lift the sights of all above the raging political controversy and the unfortunate student strike then in progress. To our amazement the chapel was filled to capacity. All walked out in absolute silence until the big clock struck. It was a lifting experience which those who participated in it will not easily forget.

After the teaching engagement in Massachusetts was completed, we returned to Indiana for the summer and soon began to prepare for another world-encircling tour. That time we had a plausible excuse in that I was invited to give, during the autumn of 1970, a week of addresses at Hong Kong Baptist College. We flew from Los Angeles to Tokyo with a one-day stop in Honolulu, where we visited my niece, Janet Kem, and her family. In Tokyo we stayed with Tetsuo and Emily Kobayashi and were reminded of the days when Emily was an Earlham student. After giving a few addresses, we went to Taipei before continuing to Hong Kong. We had some opportunity in Taiwan to observe the work of the well-organized Quaker Mission, as well as that of some other denominations.

In Hong Kong, while I was much occupied with three speeches a day, Virginia had some free time in the fabulous city. We greatly admired President Lam, who, in a very short time and with the help of his colleagues, had been able to build Hong

Kong Baptist College into a first-class institution. In my limited experience the college is one of the finest examples of the difference in human life which the Christian Mission can make. One of our human contacts made there in November 1970 has been continued by the transfer of an exceptional student, John Wong, to my Alma Mater. Though the death of President Lam was a severe blow, the college in Hong Kong is going forward under the competent leadership of President Tse, who was a member of the faculty when we visited there.

Our transportation to South Africa was by Dutch freighter, the elapsed time between Hong Kong and Durban being exactly three weeks. We valued the slow pace, with stops at Singapore, Kuala Lumpur, and Mauritius. The unhurried stop on the island of Mauritius was particularly pleasant. A few years earlier in London we had met a native of the island nation who had aroused our interest in his country. Indeed, the prospect of stopping at Mauritius was one of the chief inducements of a trip across the Indian Ocean. The Indian Ocean, however, is itself a sufficient inducement. For many days in December the weather was beautiful and the waters were untroubled. I had promised my wife not to try to do any serious writing on the ship, but I admit that I made a good many notes.

At the end of 1970 and in the beginning of 1971 we had our first truly African experience. We had already been in Egypt, as far south as Thebes, but we were well aware that what we encountered in the lower Nile valley was more Middle Eastern than African. We were convinced that in many ways Africa is the emerging continent, and we were determined to see as much of it as we could. Leaving the Dutch freighter at Durban, we traveled by land through the Transkei and along the beautiful coast of the Indian Ocean, eleven hundred miles, to Cape Town. In both Durban and Cape Town we soon had the advantage of the Christian fellowship, even though upon arrival we were total strangers in each of those big cities. An unhurried interview with the Stated Clerk of the Reformed Church of the Cape was especially gratifying.

After staying thirteen days in Cape Town, we flew to Johannesburg, where the highlight of our stay was a biracial meeting for worship in one of the suburbs. Though we did not understand one word of the language in which the hymns, prayers, and testimonies were expressed, that was no serious handicap. It encouraged us to find that the Christian fellowship could transcend the differences of race and language in a way which the political experience did not. We visited the country home of General Smuts where we were reminded of the greatness of his spirit.

In Rhodesia the grandeur of Victoria Falls exceeded our hopes. But however impressive the tumbling water may be, the memory of Dr. Livingstone is more impressive still. Time after time I returned to his monument with an overpowering sense of gratitude for the life of that brave and devoted man, who gave the African slave trade the greatest blow it ever received.

Near Bulawayo we made a special effort to see the burial place of Cecil Rhodes, to which I had been introduced years earlier in the writings of Olive Schreiner. In Kampala we visited the Archbishop of Uganda, who is a black man and a person of deep devotion. Having read Alan Moorehead's valuable book, *The White Nile*, in preparation for our visit, we thought much of explorer John Speke's visit when life in Uganda was almost totally barbarous. What filled me with wonder was the radical change which the Christian Mission has produced in a single century.

By good fortune we left Kampala shortly before the *coup* which involved some bloodshed, and which brought the present military regime to power. We were given a hint of what was about to occur when we were informed that our plane reservation for the flight to Kisumu was canceled. It was necessary to reach western Kenya because I was scheduled to lead a retreat there, but it was not easy to know how to accomplish that. When we learned that every space on the train was already assigned, we decided to try the bus, which we did, though it turned out to be a harrowing experience. Departing from Kampala at 9 P.M., we arrived at Kisumu at 6 A.M., after traveling in crowded conditions over an especially rough road. But we were glad that even a poor mode of travel was available.

Our weeks in Kenya taught us a great deal. We knew already that the East African Yearly Meeting is the world's largest regional body of Quakers, but we were not really prepared for the vitality which we observed there. The many schools and the modern hospital are impressive, and we love the students who come to us from Kenya, particularly Moses Kisuza. When we think that the Friends East African Mission is only seventy years old, we are surprised that so much could have been accomplished in so short a period. The earliest of the Quaker missionaries were clearly persons of vision and strong character.

In Nairobi, where we stayed both before and after visiting the game preserve at the foot of Mt. Kilimanjaro, our most valuable contact was that with the University of Nairobi, facilitated by our friendship with Bishop Stephen Neill. This veteran missionary statesman has made a visible impact upon his academic community, which is likely to remain, even though he has retired from his active duties. One fact which heartened us is that the entire Christian Movement is going forward rapidly in Kenya, providing one vivid bit of counterevidence to the widespread supposition that Christianity is now in a period of decline or obsolescence. By the time I left Kenya I had already decided to write a book on the World Mission, seeking to provide an intellectual answer to its critics. As stated earlier, I was able to carry the project to completion, the book being entitled *The Validity of the Christian Mission.*

About a year after our African journey we had a very pleasant five weeks in Ireland and in England. As has been possible on many other journeys, we were able to combine public service and personal pleasure because we see no incompatibility between them. My ostensible reason for a visit to Ireland in April 1972 was the invitation to give the annual lecture in Dublin at the Ireland Yearly Meeting of Friends, but we went ahead of time in order to be at Limerick and Bunratty Castle. We found the flight from Chicago to Shannon a comfortable way to go, and we enjoyed traveling from Limerick to Dublin by car. On an earlier visit we had toured Northern Ireland with its beautiful seacoast, but we limited our 1972 visit to the Republic of Ireland. At the Yearly Meeting, however, we met our old friends from Belfast and surrounding towns, who told us of the tragedies which they had suffered.

From Dublin we flew to London on May 1 and settled again at the Cora Hotel. With a minimum of engagements we had abundant time to attend concerts of the London Symphony and the London Philharmonic as well as to visit Johnson haunts near Fleet Street. Two incidents of our unhurried visit I find memorable. The first was the opportunity to give the sermon in the Cambridge University Church, when I felt it right to speak of the spiritual pilgrimage of John Woolman, a pilgrimage which ended in England two hundred years earlier. The second was my visit, on May 24, to the site of the Aldersgate Meetinghouse where, on that day in 1738, John Wesley had his revolutionary experience. From Aldersgate I walked to Bunhill Fields and was lifted as I remembered George Fox, Susanna Wesley, Daniel Defoe, John Bunyan, and Isaac Watts. Seldom have I been so conscious of the cloud of witnesses.

As we face the coming years we are making plans to revisit some places which we are eager to see again and to visit other places for the first time. Already we have promised to be in Greece for both lecturing and touring. I look forward especially to my first view of Thessalonica. Nearby I want to see where Christianity first penetrated the European Continent. Later we hope to see Iran and try to sense the resurgence of the Persian civilization. We may possibly combine a visit to Mainland China, now open to us, with one to the Soviet Union. Having been long intrigued by the vitality of Moscow Baptists, it is our expectation that the Moscow visit will be managed for us by the Baptist World Alliance.

Our present life at Richmond, when we are at home, is itself deeply satisfying. I have decided that I do not have to run to answer every telephone call, and that there is really nothing wrong with sitting on the terrace just being quietly thankful. One of our major discoveries is that it is not required of us to attend all of the meetings which occur with such frequency. We consequently spend many evenings at home, though we make some visits to nearby cities. I value my charter membership in the Indiana Academy and many other connections in Indianapolis, particularly those of Lilly Endowment, of which Landrum Bolling is now the director.

Teague Library is a source of joy every day that I am in it. Paneled in walnut, it has about it a simple beauty, while the thermopane windows exclude almost all exterior noise. My desk lamp, made of the spines of books, reminds me daily of my daughter who purchased it with her very first wages when, before her marriage, she was employed in Cincinnati. My desk dictionary reminds me of Palo Alto friends who presented it to me in 1936, the first year of our residence in California. Nearby is Roget's *Thesaurus*, purchased in Boston in 1923. A photograph of Rufus Jones, taken in his study and signed "Sincerely thy friend," is an inspiration every time I look at it.

By using a buzzer I can reach my associate, Robert Pitman, who sits in an attractive building nearby which, with its bow window, hardly suggests that it was formerly a garage. As soon as I have completed writing a chapter in a book, Mr. Pitman is usually ready to start typing it. He is able to handle this, along with the numerous letters which come each day from various points of the compass. Sometimes my wife insists on doing the entire typing of a book, and at other times she gives Mr. Pitman assistance when his burden is too heavy. If a man cannot work under these conditions, it is doubtful if he can work anywhere.

In the afternoons I work in the flower garden midway between our two small buildings. When I am not occupied with the dahlias or the vegetable garden, I work with the roses. My dahlia bulbs are the much appreciated gift of a respected Lincoln scholar, Louis A. Warren. Since there is a boy to cut the grass, I am free to give part of my afternoons to the loving care of a variety of plants. Flowers, like people, are unequal in their production, but they are quiet about it, neither complaining nor boasting. Thus they are remarkably good companions. Our chief secret is the compost pit into which goes every ounce of kitchen garbage, as well as various trimmings. In early May I put the year's accumulation of compost on the rose garden, with spectacular results. I find a deep satisfaction in sharing in creation by actually helping new soil to be made. Tom Jones and I planned our present vegetable garden as a joint project, but from now on I shall have to do it alone. On the day on which these words are being written, we are holding President Jones' Memorial Service in the Earlham Meetinghouse.

One delightful feature of the flower garden is the yoke which hangs from a horizontal arm of an ancient oak immediately over the brick walk. This yoke is a gift from Canadian Yokefellows and provides a visible reminder of a fellowship which spans the years. The oak, presumably two hundred years old, is an inspiration in itself, for, though it bears the marks of many storms, it is still alive. The top blew out long ago, but that seems to make no essential difference.

When I began writing these memoirs, the dominant note of my thinking was the metaphor of the journey, which has already been mentioned at the end of the preface. A person has made at least a start on understanding the meaning of existence when he recognizes that every life is a pilgrimage, with many twists and turns. My philosophical studies convinced me long ago that the uniqueness of human beings lies principally in their capacity as decision-makers. The work of writing is justified if any persons who face forks in their own roads are helped in making their own decisions. The best guidebook is the narrative of actual travel.

In the days before putting pen to paper I meditated much on Robert Frost's poem, "The Road Not Taken." What, I asked, if I had elected to study in a different kind of college? What if my two marriages had been with other women? What if I had decided upon a radically different career? What if I had gone to China in 1923? What if I had joined the Episcopal ministry in 1927? What if I had remained at Guilford, as I might more easily have done? Or Haverford? Or Stanford? In each case the different consequences would have been multitudinous. Such questions are, for any individual, as fascinating as they are unanswerable. Because we simply do not know, we cannot profitably guess. What each person can do, however, is to meditate upon the consequences of the decisions actually made, realizing that each decision leads to much beyond itself.

For a while I seriously considered calling my memoirs The Road Taken, but I concluded that this would suggest a greater dependence upon Frost than is actually the case. At the same time, I was much influenced by my experience on the *Philosophenweg*, above Heidelberg, and meant for a while to entitle my book The Philosopher's Way. My wife and a few other persons argued against that, however, saying it would give the wrong impression to the potential reader. I have indeed tried to be a competent philosopher, but I have never limited myself to this one discipline.

The metaphor of the journey has been particularly appealing, especially to committed Christians who are aware that in the earliest days the followers of Christ were known as Those of the

Way. That is why John Baillie entitled his brilliant introduction to Christianity *Invitation to Pilgrimage*. All literate people owe a debt in this connection to John Bunyan, his *Pilgrim's Progress* having become long ago an essential feature of our intellectual and spiritual climate. Apart from Bunyan, Lord Tweedsmuir would not have called his own memoirs *Pilgrim's Way*. What is most attractive about the entire conception of life as a journey is the widespread realization that no man walks alone. Others walk with us now, encountering some of the same problems as they proceed, and many others have trod the same general path in earlier centuries. My four shelves of devotional classics are, I recognize, filled with what are essentially guidebooks. They tell of the pitfalls on the road, and they indicate where the reward ing views are. The farther I proceed, the more I am indebted to those who have left, for me and for others, what Professor Baillie termed "finger-posts," pointing the way.

John Baillie's *A Diary of Private Prayer*, already a classic in our own century, gives, in the morning prayer for the fifth day, one of the finest expressions which I know of our indebtedness to those who walked where we now walk and who offered hints for their successors on the common path. Baillie's unforgettable prayer is as follows:

> O Thou who wast, and art, and art to come, I thank Thee that this Christian way whereon I walk is no untried or uncharted road, but a road beaten hard by the footsteps of saints, apostles, prophets, and martyrs. I thank Thee for the finger-posts and danger-signals with which it is marked at every turning and which may be known to me through the study of the Bible, and of all history, and of all the great literature of the world.

It is required of any traveler who takes this prayer seriously, as I do, that he should add, in however slight a fashion, to the literature of pilgrimage.

The writing of my memoirs at this particular time does not mean that I think my work is completed. The present time is simply a good one in which to write about the journey up to this point, attempting to do so while it is still day. Both the price and the glory of our finitude are indicated by the fact that we do not arrive; we are always on the way.

Index

164